G000273841

Joanne Peden

A Myrtle Tree For Life's Briars

"There is no such thing as a disability in God's eyes"

The Lollard Press

First published in 2010
by The Lollard Press
19 Canberra Park
BT36 7UN

www.thelollardpress.com

Printed in Northern Ireland

All rights reserved

© Joanne Peden 2010

This book is sold subject to the condition that it shall not, by way of trade or otherwise, be lent, resold, hired out, or otherwise circulated without the publisher's prior consent in any form of binding or cover other than that in which it is published and without a similar condition including this condition being imposed on the subsequent publisher.

All Scripture quotations unless otherwise indicated
are from the KJV of the Bible.

ISBN 978-0-9565361-0-5

Contents

Dedication to Beulah Smyth

This book is in memory of my Aunt Beulah, one of God's suffering saints who fought her battle with cancer with courage, strength and selflessness to the very end. Heaven gained pure treasure.

My tribute to Beulah - 'What can I say?'

So much to say about one so gentle.
So much to say about one so dear.
That my pen would run out of ink,
My eyes would run out of tear.
So much to say about our radiant jewel.

Giving and selfless like Jesus to the end.
Others first always. You poured yourself out.
In your agony you still cared for other's joy. You were an angel
     beyond a doubt.
Laying down your life for others you were everyone's friend.

Loving, truly loving. You knew love in its truest form.
Not a love of lip service, a love of action.
You were warm, affectionate, compassionate and true. Your personality
     was so catching.
You were still smiling, still bringing hope, even through your
     wildest storm.

I've never met someone as humble as yourself.
You never blew yourself up or talked with pride.
Never wanting recognition, fame or vainglory. Behind the scenes you
     were content to hide.
Knowing that the Lord sees all, the one who stored up for you your
     reward of heaven's wealth.

Never bitter. Never complaining.
Never critical, the best in others always seeing.
Never gossipy, never harsh. You were a pure Godly being.
Cheerful and positive, with you it was never raining.

The world was made a better place because you were in it.
An amazing legacy you've left us to hold.
God's word says that we spend our days as a tale being told.
You dear Beulah, your testimony was impeccable, a shining example
    to the very last bit.

I'm so glad that you're safe in glory.
So glad that you accepted Jesus as the only way there.
Your cancer's gone, death's lost its sting, no more burdens to ever bear.
Glad for your life and love. I pray that lives will continue to be touched
    by your story.

Love Always
Joanne
xo

Acknowledgements

Thank you to all the people who gave me constant encouragement while I've been writing this book! You are all so precious and without you I would never have put pen to paper! My desire is that this book will bring great comfort to those who are hurting and all you encouragers have been a huge part of this!

Thank you!

CHAPTER 1
A HOPELESS CAUSE?

Some people think that when major trials come their way that there's nowhere to turn and that their lives are no longer worth living. Some people get mad at the Lord and turn their backs on him in the eye of the storm. Some people end up bitter instead of better after life has dealt them serious blows. If you are in any of these categories, if you're struggling to just keep battling, if you've come to the conclusion that life is more darkness than light then this book is for you. Don't give up the fight, you CAN cope! I'm writing this book to encourage hearts that are weary, to encourage people who are walking through the valley of pain and sickness, to encourage those who are feeling totally crushed under the weight of things that life has thrown at them, and to encourage those who hunger and thirst to go deeper with the Lord.

For almost four years I've been living in the valley of illness. I have ME or Chronic Fatigue Syndrome as some may know it. It's an illness that leaves me extremely weak, faint and tired. It's like living on a roller coaster as I have seasons where I'm bedridden and housebound for months on end and other seasons of brief reprieve where I can get out and about a bit but I'm still mostly in the house needing to rest. Sometimes I think I'm getting better and I'm on the road to recovery and the next thing I know my body's totally crashed again and I'm right back to square one. I know what it's like to live with constant setbacks and disappointments so I want to write this book to bring comfort, hope and inspiration to others. Some may think that it would have been better if I'd waited till I was fully healed before writing. I thought that too until I heard the still small voice whisper "You have treasure in darkness. Write now."

Over the course of my illness I've struggled with a deep sense of uselessness to the Lord because I've always been an extremely active person. Before my illness set in I was never off the go. I worked full time everyday, was actively involved in my church and Child Evangelism Fellowship. It's taken me a while to learn to cope and to rest in the Lord so I want to share my journey so far with you in order to help and bless.

One month before I'd had a proper diagnosis of what was wrong with me. I was lying in bed studying my Bible. (I'd been struggling at work for almost a year with extreme weakness, fatigue and constantly feeling faint and had been for many tests. However ME is a very difficult thing to pinpoint so it took some time to rule everything else out.) That night as I lay there I received a powerful promise from the Lord:

"Instead of the thorn shall come up the fir tree, and instead of the briar shall come up the myrtle tree." Isaiah 55:13

That night as I meditated on this verse the still small voice whispered: "Joanne, you've seen and felt only thorns and briars for some time now but take heart, I will replace these some day with a fir tree and a myrtle tree. Take heart for the thorns and briars of your painful trials won't destroy you for I will establish you."

My physical body went into complete physical meltdown when I collapsed after work one day not long after I received this promise but holding on to this portion of scripture in the midst of the pain has brought a calm assurance to my spirit that the best, God's best is yet to come.

A fir tree is an evergreen. It never changes even in the wildest storm. It has a self-supporting main stem. Some take refuge in it and some small birds and insects feed on the tree. A myrtle tree is an evergreen shrub with shiny leaves. It's very beautiful and fragrant. This is what I want to be - evergreen, strong in the Lord and constantly releasing the fragrance of Christ into the lives of others.

I'm thankful that the God I serve is the God of hope! I've known his strong hand of comfort sustaining me throughout the years. There are no hopeless causes in his eyes. In this book I will be sharing journal entries written at different periods throughout my illness. I wrote the following and this poem on one of my worst days.

Joanne's Journal

Everybody's out at church. I feel overwhelmed in my spirit because I can't go. I miss it so much. My body has been in a state of extreme heaviness and fatigue all day and until now I've been sleeping solid. I wish I could get out of this bed. I refuse to let myself get down even though I want to cry. I've been reading a fictional series of books called 'Abram's Daughters' by Beverly Lewis about the Amish people over the past few days. I'm struck by Leah's deep love for the Lord and her loyalty to obeying him even though it cost her dearly. May I ever be willing to place the Lord and others before myself and let my life be a true sacrifice! I've just been reading Mark 1:31. It's the account of the healing of Peter's mother in law.

"And he came and took her by the hand, and lifted her up; and immediately the fever left her, and she ministered unto them."

I'm holding onto this tonight tightly. I know that in his time and in his own gentle way my Lord will come and take me by the hand and I will be completely lifted up from this illness. I love the words 'And she ministered unto them.' I look forward to the day when this situation I'm in is reversed and I can serve the Lord in more ways than my physical body will let me at the minute. I'm going to write a poem expressing my thoughts about this!

A HOPELESS CAUSE

"Help me." The woman cried so desperately and weak.
Her fragile body was bed-bound. Her fever was raging sore.
Family gathered around helplessly watching and it all seemed so bleak.
No seeming remedy could be found, no course of action, only a
    closed door.

Little did they know that help was on its way.
Little did they know that this was not the end.
Sadness and tears filled the room with no hint of sunshine's ray.
Little did they know that the king would soon attend and put
    this hurting soul back on the mend.

I'm sure her eyes lit up as the king of glory took her hand.
Jesus lifted her up and the fever left her.
She arose and ministered to them all thankful that once again
    she had the strength to stand.

Oh what joy filled that house!
The king's presence beautiful and the pain just a distant blur.

O Lord my King you remain the same
What you did then you can do today.
I long for you to take my hand lift me up and speak my name.
Let me like this woman be set free to serve. O Lord use this pot of clay.

Exhaustions just consumed my whole being. I'll rest now with my
   heart filled to overflowing.

Come with me on the rest of my journey and find rest in the Lord.

**"Never say never! It's when you're at your lowest that the Lord will
lift you up. Go on smile! Fill your day with hope. Think positive!
Negativity paralyses your inner strength!"**

Shirley Adams

CHAPTER 2
WHEN LIFE'S ROSES LOSE THEIR COLOUR

In regards to ME it was very difficult to get a diagnosis. I felt myself getting weaker and weaker yet every test I went for came back clear. It was so baffling and frustrating and I couldn't seem to find any answers. I kept battling on. I forced myself to work everyday and did my best to hide how weak I was feeling from my employers and co-workers. I felt like I was on a boat. I was constantly feeling faint, dizzy, and weak and had so much pain in my legs. I fought the exhaustion at work, pushing my body by keeping as active as I could. I realise now I should have admitted how I was feeling but I felt that without a diagnosis that there couldn't be anything wrong with me. Eventually one evening after work, my body totally crashed and I was in bed for months. It was at this time that I got the diagnosis of ME. Getting a diagnosis was both a relief and a shock. I was relieved to finally have a label for my mystery illness and I was also shocked as I knew a few other people with ME and knew how debilitating it could be. I felt very afraid. I kept wondering will my body ever go again. Will I ever work again? What does my future hold? I was lying down all day every day and nothing in my life seemed solid or certain anymore except the awareness of the Lord holding me close.

One night as I lay thinking, a thought occurred to me and I picked up my journal and began to write.

Joanne's Journal 2006

For some reason I can't get an incident out of my mind tonight that happened when I was at Bible College. It was one of our usual Monday night trips to the swimming pool in Lisburn. A couple of the girls that I was with decided that it would be fun to have a go at diving! So off we went to the diving pool and climbed up to the highest board. I climbed those steps totally trembling and when I got to the edge of the board I completely froze. The 'What if' syndrome entered my mind. What if I break my back trying this? What if I don't land in the water? What if I land on top of someone and hurt them? This is far too dangerous! As I stood there totally frozen I heard a small voice saying "Excuse me." It was a tiny girl of about eight or nine years old. The little girl took one big run and jumped without any hint of fear displayed on her face. This little girl had a childlike faith for she believed wholeheartedly that no harm was going to come to her. I then overcame my fears and jumped. As I soared through the air I really felt like I'd achieved something but I'd learned my lesson from that little girl. It's the same in our christian walks. We forget our call to childlike trust. We don't throw ourselves over the edge of the diving board of circumstances and care to land into the Lord's wide arms of love and drown ourselves in his presence because we develop the 'What if' syndrome! We do what I did that night at the swimming pool. The waters beneath me were so vast that there was no chance of missing the water yet fear paralyses our bodies. In my circumstance at the minute I'm right at the edge of the diving board. I know that my Lord is able just like I knew that the water was vast enough to catch me. I know I'm in the Lord's care and "I shall not want" just like I knew that the swimming pool was littered with life guards. I know Jesus wants me to get lost in him till the waters of his love are way above my head. I've even climbed the steps by striving with all the courage I can muster to overcome my fears but every time I'm about to jump into the Lord's arms and wholly lean on him the 'What If' syndrome kicks in, What if this illness takes over my life? What if the Lord chooses not to heal me? Instead of jumping into the Lord's arms the tears come and I climb right back down those steps into a shallow pool of defeat where a deep sense of uselessness robs me of every ounce of hope in the Lord.

Matthew 18:3 says: *"Verily I say unto you, Except ye be converted, and become as little children, ye shall not enter into the kingdom of heaven."*

The Lord wants me to have the same kind of faith as that little girl on the diving board had that night. He wants me to throw myself upon him without depending on my reasoning and without shrinking back in fear and considering all that could go wrong. He's saying:

"Trust in the Lord with all thine heart; and lean not unto thine own understanding. In all thy ways acknowledge him, and he shall direct thy paths." Proverbs 3:5-6

The devil wants us to live our lives trusting in ourselves. He knows if he can get us to try and work it out ourselves and lose sight of the strength and power of our Lord, we will live our whole lives climbing right back down those steps and living in defeat and shallowness missing all that the Lord has in store for us because we failed to be as a little child. I want to be effective for my Lord. I want to triumph over this illness. I want to depend on the Lord the way that he wants me to and have a childlike trust. I'm not there yet but it's where I need to be. I can't live another day trying to figure it out by myself. I want to go right over the edge of that diving board tonight...

A few nights later a friend of mine phoned. I found her words so encouraging. She talked about how my life may seem very black and white at the moment but that colour would return. I wrote this poem based on that thought:

WHEN LIFE'S ROSES LOSE THEIR COLOUR

Red rose, pink rose, yellow rose
Where have you gone?
You've been replaced by a dull dreary black and white.
You're lifeless, limp and forlorn.

O what is this place wherein I dwell Lord?
Colourless, bleak and grey.
When will I see blue skies, red roses and rainbows?
I yearn to be lost in their bright array.

Colour my life with hope dear Lord.
Like a child's bright crayons on a blank page.
The past is gone, my present's a nightmare and my future's inconceivable.
Please unlock the door of my cage.

Help me in the eye of the storm to battle harder.
Don't let me sink in darkness. Hold me tight.
Help me to believe in light even in its absence.
No matter what, don't let me give up the fight.

Colour never returns to a corpse.
But I am very much alive.

So colour this your rose my Jesus,
That I may serve your purposes here on earth before at heaven's
  gates I arrive.

During this first physical crash I received another beautifully reassuring promise from my Lord and I recorded my thoughts into my journal. Losing your physical health causes you to grieve for the person you used to be. I no longer recognised myself so at just the right time the Lord poured fresh hope into my weary spirit!

"And I will give her her vineyards from thence, and the valley of Achor for a door of hope: and she shall sing there, as in the days of her youth, and as in the day when she came up out of the land of Egypt." Hosea 2:15

Wow! What a beautiful scripture! How come I've studied this book so many times and it's only now that it's jumping out at me! The Lords promised to open a door of hope for the valley of Achor! I'm not 100% sure what the valley of Achor was but I'm anxious to look into it right now!

Joshua 7:24-26 records more about it. It was the place where Achan and his family were stoned. A place of trouble, bloodshed and heartbreak. I feel like my heart and life are in the valley of Achor at the minute. The heavy boulders of failure, the sharp edged stones of deep disappointment, and the rocks of despair are being hurled at me and I'm feeling crushed under their weight.

Isaiah 65:10 says: *"And Sharon shall be a fold of flocks, and the valley of Achor a place for the herds to lie down in, for my people that have sought me."*

Wow! What a thought! Imagine the change when the valley of Achor becomes like a plain. A place of stillness and quietness. Where the cattle can lie down in peace. A place of blessing and joyfulness. My valley of Achor is going to become a peaceful plain, a place of nourishment, rest, shelter and hope. I want the Lord to use me to bring hope to others.

Another thought has just occurred to me. Why do people end up in the valley of Achor? Achan ended up in this place of sore trouble because of his own sin. It was his lies, unfaithfulness, deceit and wrong living that put him there. Some like Achan, are in Achor reaping the consequences of what they've sown. However, Achan's family ended up in Achor too. They were innocent, but were reaping the consequences of another's sin. Maybe you're reading this book and you've always been so faithful to the Lord but now the hard rocks are coming at you with such force that you're doubled over in agony seeing no point in living, dizzy with blood loss and helplessness. Maybe sickness has invaded your own or one of your relatives bodies and you're asking "Why me?" Pain is the consequence of living in a fallen world, a world not as God intended but marred by Adam and Eve's sin. It's not your fault but right now you're feeling so hopeless. Maybe your Achor is abuse. You keep a mask on to the world but inside your heart is breaking. It's you who feels the hard slaps against your cheeks. You take all the downgrading criticism. You feel like mud, lifeless and worthless. Maybe this is from a spouse or maybe it's unending emotional abuse at work from a colleague or manager. The valley of Achor's grip on you is so tight. You too like Achan's family are trapped by somebody else's sin. Maybe you're at the point where your hot tears saturate your pillow at night. Maybe it's got to the point where you're grasping for control. You've stopped eating and you live under a constant shadow of guilt and condemnation. There seems to be no escape from the pain. Maybe you're in the Achor of broken dreams. You've miscarried that precious child you longed for. Maybe your fiancé has broken off your engagement. Maybe you've failed at something that you worked so hard to achieve. You gave 100% and then the critic was raised up against you and suddenly everything spiralled out of control. Maybe the boulders of failure have smashed against you and you're lying in a fragmented state. All of a sudden life's lost its purpose. Maybe your Achor is financial turmoil. Maybe it's emotional disturbances like depression or panic attacks. Maybe it's the agony over a wayward child.

Yes, you are in the valley of Achor, of pain, hurt, abuse, tears and you feel trapped. You feel like you've been thrown into a dungeon and someone's thrown away the key. The sickness seems to be lasting too long. The hurt seems unending. Your grief for your loved one seems endless. That relationship feels like someone's put you on the gallows with a huge rope around your neck and slowly you're choking, you're suffocating, it's so overpowering.

The Lord's offering you exactly the same as he's offering me. 'A door of hope for the valley of Achor.' Maybe you're desperately looking around trying to find this door but Jesus is saying "I AM" that door and I'm going to bring you through to a place where you will sing again, where you'll find yourself in an abundant vineyard in the Lord and you will marvel at how he turned things around. Cling to this promise in faith along with me when all seems lost. The Lord is going to use your negative experiences to create opportunities that you never dreamt possible. Your valley of Achor will become that place of calm. The latter part of Isaiah 65:10 tells us *"For my people have sought me."* Keep crying out to him; don't let the pain numb you or a root of bitterness settle in your heart. Keep crying out to our beloved Lord in childlike trust in your own simple way. Keep giving him the cream of your heart in worship even in your agony and in due season he'll lift you up to a place that only your Achor prepared you for. A place where your relationship with the Lord is deeper and where you are consumed with desire for him and him alone.

Just maybe you've picked up this book and you're not a Christian. Yet you are dwelling in a very broken place and can find no rest or peace. Jesus can be your door of hope, he died for you and he longs for you to come to him. If you'll turn and yield your life to him, he will save you. He'll save you from an eternity in hell and you'll never again have to fear death. You'll have an absolute certainty that you'll have an eternity in heaven of bliss and unending joy in your Lord's presence. You'll also have an assurance of the Lord's daily strength and closeness to see you through every Achor. I'm not saying that if you become a Christian your illness will go away or all of a sudden your spouse or manager or critic is going to fall at your feet and sing your praises. In fact your Achor may continue but you will have the assurance of a door of hope and that the Lord that you now love will never put you through more than you can bear for he is compassionate and loving. I hope that these simple thoughts on this verse will encourage you in your wildest storm.

This first physical crash of mine was painful and so many days my journal read 'Help me Lord I'm drowning.' However, eventually after months of being housebound I picked up enough strength to go to church and short trips through the week! The Lord truly didn't permit me to go through any more than I could possibly have borne! Getting out to church for the first time after months in bed was like every dream coming true at once. It was like a cool drink reviving my spirit on a hot summer's day; it was bliss to be among people once again! It was the first glimmer of a door of hope, the first glimmer of life's roses regaining their colour!

"God has a prison ministry. He explodes the walls of impossibility."

T.D. Jakes

CHAPTER 3
NOT CREATED IN VAIN

As a child I really loved playing the board game 'Snakes and Ladders.' We spent many hours playing this game. It can be a very frustrating game though because just when you think you're going to win the game you land on a nasty snake and find yourself near the beginning of the board. All of a sudden you're losing! Having ME is like living one's life on a snakes and ladders board. You think you're winning, you've overcome obstacles, gone to a higher plain health wise and you think you're about to beat it when all of a sudden you crash and slide right back down the slippery slope. You find yourself beginning to lose the battle.

Life's roses were beginning to regain their colour and I was able to be out and about more often. Then my Aunt Beulah began to lose her battle with cancer. Beulah had put up an amazing fight. Over the four years of fighting the illness I never heard her complain once. She was bubbly, bright, strong in God and so considerate of other people's needs. I'm really thankful that my body let me go to the hospital for a couple of hours every day during her final weeks on earth. Even though she was in agony in those final weeks she was still putting others before herself. One day as I sat with her she opened her eyes and looked at me and told me to go home for I looked exhausted. On another occasion when the pastor was leaving he told her everyone was praying for her. Beulah's response was 'Don't pray for me, pray for them.' Beulah was referring to the family that she was going to leave behind. She had a Christ like, selfless spirit even to her dying day. When Beulah passed away it was heartbreaking but at the same time triumphant for since she loved the Lord we knew that she went straight to be with her Lord in paradise, fully healed and no longer in pain.

My body had started to get weaker and weaker because of the increased activity that it couldn't cope with and two weeks after the funeral my body totally crashed again and I was in bed and housebound for another few months. Before I record some of my journal entries and share with you all the precious nuggets of strength and hope that the Lord poured into my spirit at this time I'd like to talk briefly about bereavement.

Maybe you're reading this book and your life is a struggle because you've lost someone you love. Maybe you feel like you buried a massive part of yourself when they lowered that casket into the ground. There's heaviness in your heart, a constant ache and a barren scalding sense of loneliness. You wonder how you'll ever live without your loved one and every time you look around you see constant reminders of them. Remember as you wade through the thick briars of bereavement the Lord is standing with you holding out a myrtle tree of hope. I took great comfort from Psalm 146:5-7b&8.

"Blessed is he that hath the God of Jacob for his help, whose hope is in the Lord his God ... The Lord looseth the prisoners: The Lord openeth the eyes of the blind: the Lord raiseth them that are bowed down: the Lord loveth the righteous."

The Lord is our help in our prisons of pain and loss. He truly does raise up spirits that are bowed down, he covers us in his love as we grieve and weep. The Lord laid this poem on my heart and writing it brought me great comfort. Death has NO sting left in its tail for those who die prepared!

"I KNOW WHERE YOU ARE"

My Child I know what you're feeling
I have been there myself.
Losing Lazarus caused my heart to break, tears to fall, great pain
and anguish.
Don't be afraid to release your emotion for I the king of glory
released mine.

A lifetime of memories flashes through your mind my child.
I had my memories too.
Sweet fond memories of togetherness and joy.
That are very precious.

But I the King of Glory couldn't stand by on the sidelines.
I couldn't see my friend robbed of life.
From the tomb I commanded him to come out.
He emerged full of vitality.

That's what I love to do. To put the grave back in its place.

I have conquered death; it's had its last say.
Your loved one who loved me has emerged from the tomb.
Now he stands with me triumphant.

So my child as you grieve and weep.
Missing your loved one's presence.
Remember I am with you, holding you and giving you strength.
I AM your Lord.

The passage referred to in this poem is John chapter 11.

The Lord was still leading me to a place of fresh hope even though I found myself in total relapse once again. However my initial reaction to going back to this place of total inactivity was as follows.

Joanne's Journal

I'm so frustrated and the Lord seems ten million miles away at this moment in time. I've gone down again big time into another dip. Yesterday was scary. I got out of bed and was on my way to the bathroom when I collapsed on the floor. When I came round I managed to get up but I collapsed again and banged my head against the wall. This time I couldn't get up and had to creep slowly to the phone to ring for help. I'm really afraid my body is like this because I tried to go out for two hours everyday. I'm 24 years old and my body's weak, frail and dysfunctional. My future looks bleak, empty and black. Will I always have a disabled body? Lord Jesus please help me!

That night I drew strength from 1 John 5:4; *"For whatsoever is born of God overcometh the world: and this is the victory that overcometh the world, even our faith."*

I didn't feel like an overcomer but feelings lie. They scream the opposite of whatever the Bible is saying. I recorded my heart's cry because every time I tried to pray I got so exhausted that I lost concentration.

"Darling Lord. My concentration is so broken and my spirit is so downcast. I feel totally deflated. Is my life going to be an empty existence of not even being able to be 100% committed to things at church, of not being strong enough to be out two hours everyday without going into physical meltdown? I feel so scared. O Lord what's the use of questions. All I know is that I've loved you passionately from a very young age and only want your way. Lord if this is the way for my life would you grant me grace to accept it? Or if you're going to heal me please bring the full deliverance that I need. Help me to bring you glory every day even from my sickbed. In these awful valley days, don't let me slip into despair. Keep me safe and bring me through. Lord your word says tonight that you've given me victory to overcome the world through faith. Shield me from the god of this world, 'Satan' as I lie here. Don't let me swallow his lies and don't let me doubt you. I ask for your power to overcome. Help me to rest secure in the knowledge that my own church and close friends from many denominations are constantly lifting me up to your throne. Thank you that even in my brokenness you love me. I love you so much too."

The Lord never created anyone in vain no matter how ill or how limited they may be. This poem sums up my feelings from this time. It's based on the creation account in Genesis chapter one and Isaiah 45:18. Part of this verse in Isaiah reads *"he created it not in vain."* I'm not created in vain! My life has so much more meaning than I can possibly imagine at the minute.

NOT CREATED IN VAIN

Without form, void and totally dark.
No glimmer of hope and apparent waste.
No colour, no light, just a thick black paste.
Such was the scene in the beginning.

Not just back then but right now dear Lord.
I feel like my life is in vain. Everything seems so bleak.
I'm cocooned and can't break free from a body that is tired and weak.
In the silence I wonder 'Am I created in vain?'

Then the miracle of life bursts through the gloom.
"The Spirit of God moved."

What sweet relief, what aching fears at once are soothed
As your breath of life covers me.

I anticipate that day with great longing.
I can't wait to hear your voice speaking "Light."
My life will be fresh, new and dazzling white.
You speak and bring things to pass that I know for sure.

No, this is NOT in vain for you make no mistakes.
I have a call and destiny yet to be fulfilled.
Like a butterfly I'll emerge, darkness gone and fears all stilled.
Let me be what you made me to be.

Throughout this period I did all I could to stay positive and let hope keep rising within me. One night I lay in bed thinking how much I used to enjoy a funfair. I recorded this thought in my journal.

Joanne's Journal

I love funfairs so much. I love the waltzers and being spun around so quickly. I love the dodgems and crashing into people in a world where there are no rules. I love the ghost train and laughing at those daft ghosts that look so fake! I love the ice cream and bright lights. This made me think of life. The funfair days will live again. Life's about joy as well as sorrow. I've known so much sorrow so I'm going to believe that the waltzer days of spinning around in excitement accomplishing things for the Lord are just ahead. *"[Joanne] SHALL reap if she faints not!"* Galatians 6:9

The next promise I received came at night time. It felt like a warm blanket surrounding me on a cold night.

Joanne's Journal

Today has been a nightmare day physically but I'm trying to rest in the knowledge that my Lord is still in all and over all. He is still sovereignly reigning from his throne even though my life seems so dull. I felt a bit trapped earlier; all childhood dreams seemed to be shattered. My Lord knows how I feel but glory to his name he is still Lord over all my life and he still has a plan.

Wow! I've just been reading Isaiah 62:4! What perfect timing! *"Thou shalt no more be termed Forsaken; neither shall thy land any more be termed Desolate: but thou shalt be called Hephzi-bah, and thy land Beulah: for the Lord delighteth in thee, and thy land shall be married."*

What's my Lord saying to his broken child tonight? Hephzibah means "My delight is in her." According to Matthew Henry Hephzibah was the name for Hezekiah's queen (2 Kings 21:1), it was the proper name for a wife who ought to be her husband's delight (Proverbs 5:19). The church's maker is her husband.

"For thy Maker is thine husband; the Lord of hosts is his name; and thy Redeemer the Holy One of Israel; The God of the whole earth shall he be called." Isaiah 54:5

"She shall be called Beulah, which signifies married, whereas she had been desolate, a condition opposed to that of the married wife. *'Thy land shall be married,'* that is, it shall become fruitful again and be replenished. Though she has long been barren, she shall again be peopled, shall again be made to keep house and to be a joyful mother of children."[1] (Psalm 113:9)

This has brought me so much comfort tonight. It's a joy to know that my Lord's delight is in me even though I can offer him so little at the minute. The word *forsaken* means: "A place completely deserted, a person left absolutely alone or helpless."

Desolate means: "Deserted, uninhabited, barren, lifeless, devastated, laid waste, forlorn or hopeless, extremely unhappy."

These words are exactly how I've been feeling today! Helpless, barren and hopeless. The words 'laid waste' describes it best but glory to the name of my Lord tonight that he has promised that I shall no longer be termed forsaken or desolate but my Lord's bringing me to my 'Beulah land.' The place of fulfilment. He's bringing me to a place of greater fruitfulness where I'll bring him much delight and where he'll multiply me. My life's not always going to be a constant battle with sickness and

I've got to cling tight to this in these barren empty days! What a promise! There's a cross reference to Jeremiah 32:41. I'm going to personalise it and hold onto it.

"Yea, I will rejoice over [Joanne] to do [her] good and I will plant [Joanne] in this land assuredly with my whole heart and with my whole soul."

I love this quote from Matthew Henry: "Wherever God's children are they are still upon their father's ground so they are still under their father's eye and care. They may lose themselves in a wilderness but God has not lost them."[2]

I'm looking forward to the day where my wailing is turned into dancing and the day where my sackcloth is removed and in its place are robes of joy! Psalm 30:11

...A few days later I wrote a song and hummed a tune for it as I lay in bed. This truly is the song of my heart to my Shepherd today. It's been a day where the hot tears have been flowing, where I've felt lonely and had an empty ache in my heart. Though all afternoon I've had this unbelievable sense of the Lord wrapping me tightly in his arms and helping me through!

SHEPHERD OF MY SOUL

Shepherd of my soul.
Hide me under your strong arm.
Shepherd of my soul.
Without you I'm lost and alone.
Here I am precious comforter
Afraid, tired and worn.
Shepherd of my soul protect your child today.

Chorus
For I love you, I love you. To you alone I cleave.
I thank-you, I thank-you for your mercy I receive.
Precious Lord I'm glad for Calvary, that by your stripes I am healed.
Shepherd of my soul I give my all to you.

I wasn't created in vain. The illness didn't mark the end in fact it opened a new door to a closer walk with my Lord. Physical crash two ended and again I had a season of brief reprieve. I'd like to focus on the blessings of this brief period in the next chapter!

"When you have a setback, don't take a step back. Get ready for the come back."

Author Unknown

CHAPTER 4
THE CALM BEFORE THE STORM

My worst storm was yet to come but for three months I knew a greater sense of freedom physically. I really thought that I was beating my illness at this point. So come with me and experience along with me what I learned in this brief reprieve.

Joanne's Journal

I feel so alive today! I met with God afresh in the middle of the night! I'm excited about today! I'm turning 25 and over the past while the thief has come to steal and destroy and now's the time to lift up my head and move forward! I'm fighting back and I'm determined to beat this illness. I had such a beautiful day and my heart is overflowing with thankfulness for what my body allowed me to do today. I praise and thank my Lord for strength in my legs to get out of bed and for the friend who came and took me to Portstewart for lunch. I couldn't stop smiling. Going to lunch in Portstewart probably wouldn't seem very exciting to someone healthy, but for me it meant a couple of hours release from the house. It meant feeling like a person for a while instead of an illness. It was lovely to enjoy laughter and warm conversation, to go down to the beach and paddle in the sea and to eat ice-cream while watching the world go by! What an amazing day and what an amazing Lord I serve. Today I dwelt in a place of beauty in the midst of pain. This day has been completely owned and blessed of God. I never imagined being strong enough for such a day even a month ago so my hearts bursting and I'm returning praise to God. Deuteronomy 7:15 has encouraged my heart even more!

"And the Lord will take away from thee all sickness." Also Psalm 138:8 *"The Lord will perfect that which concerneth me: thy mercy, O Lord, endureth forever: forsake not the works of thine own hands."*

I'm going to rest now and let these words from God's lips strengthen my heart as I meditate upon them.

Another amazing thing happened during this period. I was strong enough for a few weeks to return to Girls' Brigade and teach the scripture course for an hour each Wednesday night. My brief period of being back at GB was such an amazing blessing to me. It was a joy to be part of a team again! It gave me back a sense of normality! It was a joy to be teaching the girls again, it was a joy to be able to do something practical in God's service once again. After the first night back I recorded in my journal:

> "What an amazing day! I got GB restored to me tonight! I can't believe what God's restoring to me! I have a long way to go physically but I'm thankful for glorious baby steps in the right direction."

This poem that I've written speaks about how the sun is still shining 'Just beyond the clouds.'

JUST BEYOND THE CLOUDS

Foggy, dismal, dark and grey.
That's the picture that greeted me from my window today.
There's not even a glimpse of a single sunny ray.
Heavy rain is falling. It's coming down without delay.

Though it's all so colourless, dull and bare.
In the distance the birds are still singing like they haven't got a care.
Just beyond the clouds the sun still shines like a precious treasure O so rare.
It will shine in the grey places once again in answer to every prayer.

Just beyond the clouds of life's harsh trials and pain,
God's promises stand true. He'll turn winter into spring again.
Keep expectant and looking to God with tiny faith like a mustard grain.
Treasure for darkness will appear turning your heaviness into blessing
    and gain.

During these few weeks I really could see rays of sunshine coming from beyond the clouds. Even though I had so many physically bad days during this period the good days far outweighed the bad. I really enjoyed going visiting on better days. I just wanted to give back some of the love that had been poured into me. These days were such a huge blessing. Over this period my Bible studies mainly focused on 'developing a heart of greater compassion.'

One day I was reading 2 Timothy 1:4; *"Greatly desiring to see thee, being mindful of thy tears, that I may be filled with joy".*

Timothy cried tears of compassion and pain when he saw Paul being arrested and afflicted with chains. Paul didn't rebuke Timothy's tears as being unmanly or he doesn't give any indication that there was no place for emotion in Christianity.

JH Jowett wrote: "Tearless hearts can never be heralds of the passion. When our sympathy loses its pang we can no longer be servants of the passion."

"Lord, give me Timothy's tears of compassion for those in chains of sickness or any other trial. Lord forbid that my heart ever becomes harsh and tearless, uncompassionate and selfish. Increase my compassion Lord Jesus and give me a heart like yours. The song says 'You had no tears for you own grief's but sweat drops of blood for mine.' I'd rather cry tears of compassion for others than tears of self-pity or tears of frustration. I'm so unlike you Lord. Increase my love."

Reflecting on this period some simple yet profound life lessons strike me:

1 To appreciate and be thankful for every single day and to enjoy every blessing.

2 To enjoy the preciousness of quality time with family and friends.

3 To live expectantly and obediently to the Lord even when life seems uncertain. Like Anna in Luke 2:37-38 *"And she was a widow of about fourscore and four years, which departed not from the temple, but served God with fastings and prayers night and day."* Anna had the joy of seeing the Messiah come. Her faithfulness was rewarded and she was blessed to see the first glimmer of light in the darkness.

4 To take nothing for granted. I didn't know whether I was going to have good days or bad days so I made the most of every single outing!

5 To be secure in the knowledge that the Lord holds all the missing pieces to the jigsaw of my life. It's too easy for me to become

discontented and wonder when I will be able to work again and try and put time limits on the Lord but he's shown me that in his time the missing pieces will fall into place and the picture will be so clear.

Reflecting on this period inspired me to yet again pick up my pen and write a poem. I've entitled it:

THE CALM BEFORE THE STORM

The sea is a picture of undisturbed tranquillity. The sky is the purest, clearest shade of blue.
Children's laughter echoes around the beach as they build sandcastles in the sand.
Couples deeply in love come walking at a leisurely pace hand in hand.
The cafes around the pier echo with warm conversation as people gather over fish and chips or homemade stew.

A grey cloud now hovers over the sky though no one seems aware.
The merriment continues. Kites are being flown, balls are bouncing and there's a long queue at the ice-cream van.
Sunbathers are starting to feel the sudden chill and abandon their desires to get a tan.
The sea is growing choppier and a slight breeze ruffles the people's hair.

The sky is completely black now and the rain is falling fast like a mighty waterfall.
The laughter's died down as people run to their cars and shops for refuge.
The strong winds begin to growl like a hungry bear and the crashing waves are huge.
The beach is almost empty now apart from the candy floss man desperately trying to dismantle his stall.

What a completely different scene now appears before our eyes.
The calmness has been pierced by upheaval, noise and stress.
Things that have been left behind in haste now clutter the beach leaving a mess.
Lips that not too long ago echoed merry chat now echo disappointment and loud sighs.

This period of my life was like the calm before my wildest storm.
Little did I know what was just ahead. Just like those carefree people
   on the beach that day.
My Lord knew the skies where about to change but I was safe within his
   embrace. Secure in his arms I lay.
Through the bitter, icy winds of calamity no harm befell me for he kept
   me safe and warm.

Another thing that was on my heart during this period was to keep
submitting to God no matter what he asked of me. For a long time during
this period I was studying the life of Mary in my quiet times.

*"And Mary said, Behold the handmaid of the Lord; be it unto me according to
thy word. And the angel departed from her."* Luke 1:38. Also *"For he hath
regarded the low estate of his handmaiden: for, behold, from henceforth all
generations shall call me blessed."* Luke 1:48. The dictionary defines Hand
maiden as a 'Female servant' - someone whose essential function is to
serve or assist. Mary describes herself as a 'Doule' or a slave girl. Complete
obedience marked out a Doule and they are described as someone who did
fully the will of the master.

The Believer's Bible commentary says: "In beautiful submission, Mary yielded
herself to the Lord for the accomplishment of his wondrous purpose."[3]

It's easy to sing "All to Jesus I surrender" but do we really mean it? As
a young Christian when I sang or spoke these words I imagined God
using me in a big way. However in reality I was abandoning myself to
God's purposes even though it held a long path of pain. Not exactly the
romanticised notions I had previously! It's easy for me to think at times
over the years that this illness has rendered me not much use to God but
when I think like this I forget that I've totally surrendered all to God and
his leading me this way is no accident.

One of my favourite fiction books is called "Not my will. How much will
surrender cost" by Francena H Arnold. One of my favourite quotes in it
is: "Christ's - for service or sacrifice."[4]

So often we struggle with God and postpone our submission. Mary had reasons not to submit. She didn't understand, she was afraid, she knew the penalty for pregnancy outside marriage was death; she could lose her husband to be. However in quiet heroism this great girl of faith submitted willingly and without all the answers to God's mysterious will. In essence Mary was saying 'I live to serve you, I desire no life apart from you, and I will do whatever you ask because I belong to you. I will do whatever you ask quietly and without question. Let it be to me according to your word.' It's a massive thing to say "Lord whatever you throw at me I'm fine with that" because we have no idea what's going to come. Though I know right now I'm just where he wants me to be this is not where I want to be but if going deeper with God means hard trials then I want to endure them.

The prayer I recorded in my journal reflects a flesh verses spirit reaction to what I'd been studying.

"Lord I'm not very good at submitting humbly to your will. I fight against it, question it, become troubled by it, I strive and I look to the flesh. Some days I don't see a way out of this illness. How many more crashes are in front of me? I don't want to go to that place again. I really do believe your promises but I guess like Mary I struggle to see the performance. I understand that you can. It's the how that I struggle with. Lord instill in me a spirit of humility like Mary's. Strip me bare of strong will and self-dependency. I want to be a handmaiden. I'm not obeying you as I ought in my strivings. Help me to be a woman of great faith like Mary, submitting humbly to you even though I don't have all the answers. Even if obeying you doesn't mean instant healing 'Still I will follow.' I truly desire no life apart from you and I know that whatever you've promised will come to pass. Help me to stop striving and fill me with your peace." Love Joanne xo

Maybe you're reading this and you're not a Christian and you're thinking if giving my heart to the Lord means pain I think I'll just hold onto my heart and keep sitting on the fence. I would urge you to remember that this life is over in the twinkling of an eye yet eternity is forever. Heaven or hell is your choice but the Lord longs for you to be his and choose him and heaven. Hard things hit both Christians and non Christians but with Jesus on our side things are easier to bear because he gives us fresh strength and more of him everyday! Don't battle alone!

Christian don't be afraid to surrender all even in the hard times.

"Blessed be God, even the Father of our Lord Jesus Christ, the Father of mercies, and the God of all comfort; Who comforteth us in all our tribulation, that we may be able to comfort them which are in any trouble, by the comfort wherewith we ourselves are comforted of God. For as the sufferings of Christ abound in us, so our consolation also aboundeth by Christ." 2 Corinthians 1:3-5

As the hill I was climbing was about to get steeper I had the assurance of the Lord's comfort surrounding me. As you join me on my steep climb keep in mind one of the verses of the old hymn 'Blessed Assurance'. "Perfect Submission all is at rest. I in my Saviour am happy and blessed. Watching and waiting looking above. Filled with his goodness lost in his love."

"Sometimes life is so hard you can only do the next thing. Whatever that is just do the next thing. God will meet you there."

Elizabeth Elliot

CHAPTER 5
RAGDOLL

My next physical crash was one of my worst. For almost two months I lay in bed with no signs of improvement whatsoever. In fact every day I was getting worse. I was passing out too many times to even keep track off. One night I lay holding on tight to a couple of scriptures I'd received at the beginning of the crash.

"For thou hast been a strength to the poor, a strength to the needy in his distress, a refuge from the storm, a shadow from the heat, when the blast of the terrible ones is as a storm against the wall." Isaiah 25:4. Also *"The glorious Lord will be to us as a wide river of protection, and no enemy can cross."* Isaiah 33:21 (Living Bible). These verses were as manna to my soul. Even though I felt awful I reminded myself that the Lord was my shadow from the heat and my wide river of protection. After thinking things were being restored to me I initially grieved once again because of the things that I could no longer do. My initial journal entry reflected this.

Joanne's Journal

Hard. It's a hard place that I'm in today. It's hard to cope with the disappointment of a dilapidated body once again. It's hard to lie in bed all day and wish with every ounce of my being that I was out and about. I'm totally exhausted and weak. I was so looking forward to being well for Christmas this year and now it's not looking like it. I've just poured out my heart to the Lord and told him where I am."

Someone had sent me a little daily reading pamphlet at that time. I've no idea what it was called or who it was by but that day as I opened it I really received strength from the Lord. *"When the priests who are carrying the ark touch the water with their feet the river will stop flowing as though held back by a dam and will pile up as though against an invisible wall! Now it was the harvest season and the Jordan was overflowing at its banks."* Joshua 3:13-14a (Living Bible)

The little pamphlet said: "Have you ever noticed that the Lord does some of his best work when the floods of life are raging? Here he instructed the people of Israel to cross the Jordan River at flood stage, not when the waters were low simply because he wanted them to realise that it was his power not their efforts that allowed them to taste victory. Never forget that God works best in flood situations."

This was the Lord's answer to my uncertainty. I felt that my life was in a flood situation. The rivers of suffering were overflowing their banks but I believed my God was much more than able to step in his way and time, I cried out to him "Lord get me through this river so I can live sold out to you with energy to burn."

A few days later I was reading Zephaniah 3:19 and I was so inspired by C.H Spurgeon's prayer. *"I will save her that halteth."*

"Lord though I halt in faith, in prayer, in praise, in service and in patience, save me I beseech thee. Only thou can save such a cripple as I am. Lord let me not perish because I am among the hindmost but gather me up by thy grace the slowest of thy pilgrims – even me." (Spurgeon). Dwelling on the prayer of this great man of faith and spiritual leader really encouraged my weary soul that day.

I was getting weaker. The climax of being rushed to hospital was coming but I clung to God with all that was within me. Just a week before Christmas my journal read as follows:

Joanne's Journal

Even though I was a physical mess today God's peace did surround my mind. I read Mark 8:22-25;

"And he (Jesus) took the blind man by the hand... and when he had spit on his eyes, and put his hands upon him, he asked him, if he saw aught. And he looked up, and said 'I see men as trees, walking.' After that he put his hands upon his eyes, and made him look up: and he was restored and saw every man clearly."

This really hit me. I thought why did Jesus have to touch him twice? Why did he only partially heal him at first when he healed other people in an instant? I knew deep in my heart that the Lord wanted to speak to me through this but I was so baffled. I looked up the notes in the Life Application Bible and it made it so clear!

"The miracle was not too difficult for Jesus, but he chose to do it in stages, possibly to show the disciples that some healings would be gradual rather than instantaneous or to demonstrate that spiritual truth is not always perceived clearly at first. Before Jesus left, however the man was healed completely."[5]

What's being said to me through this? With the touch of God's hand I could be 100% well tomorrow but I'm going on a journey of faith with him first even though it's hard. If the Lord gives me partial healing like I had before I'm not to be scared but to hide in my heart that some day the same touch of the master that gives partial healing also in his time and after the lessons have been learned brings total restoration!

Christmas day Journal entry:

I haven't written in here for a few days. I've been at my absolute worst. I've been fainting constantly... Christmas Eve was the bleakest darkest day I've ever had. I lay and listened to carols on Classic FM all day with many a tear shed for I felt so helpless. I woke this morning and just felt so numb. It took every ounce of strength left within me to open my presents but they brought lots of smiles. They made a dark day so much brighter. Everyone has been so kind to me. Family, friends and people from church. Their thoughtfulness has inspired fresh fight in me today. I'm thankful too that this day is a celebration of our only hope in this world - my precious Jesus!

The New Year passed much the same as Christmas. A close friend of mine gave me a testimony CD, of a man called George McMurty from Bangor Elim. This man had suffered from five strokes and spoke from his heart about how difficult life had been. He also went on to tell about how the Lord had completely healed him. I listened to this on New Year's Eve and it gave me so much hope. I hid it in my heart in the dark days that followed.

I'd also received a book from another close friend and it also brought me much inspiration. It was called "The Brontë's: Veins running fire." It was an amazing book about a family in the 18th century who left the world a better place. Charlotte Brontë compared her journey in it to Moses when he stood on the mountain looking into the Promised Land. She talked about being firmly rooted in the life of faith and not letting circumstances stifle her creativity.

It was said of Charlotte Brontë, that she went through much pain and lived with an unshakeable depression yet she rose above it all to make her life count. She just didn't curl up and die when things went wrong. Her faith was strong. She dared to stand like Moses on the mountain rooted in a life of faith. It was a life that saw little blessing but constant pain and hardships yet she dared to let hope rise within her and look to the Promised Land where the rivers of the life of imagination flow. Charlotte wrote many books reflecting the teachings of the Bible lived out through fictional characters. Adversity didn't ruin her! Reading this when I was in a place of utter weakness spoke to me about just how the Lord can take a life that's bruised and battered and still use them for his glory. When you lie in bed all day there are times when you wonder 'What's my life really accomplishing?' but this really helped me to keep pressing through the fog and visualise a better day.

The Hospital

Exactly one week after I'd been so inspired by that book my body deteriorated even further. It was a Saturday and I'd fainted that morning and was very weak. This was nothing new as I'd been like this everyday. No one was at home and I was tucked up in bed. All of a sudden, I felt stabbing pains in my chest and found myself struggling to breathe. I grabbed the phone and rang for help. When my father got to me I was fighting for breath and drifting into unconsciousness. I remember feeling really afraid and I don't remember much else. The ambulance came and I was taken to hospital and put on oxygen. The only explanation for that day was that my body had got so weak that something as simple as breathing had become to big a strain for me. I reflect on that day still glorifying God for his amazing care for me. Help came when I needed it most!

Prayer took on new meaning in the hospital. My body had deteriorated to a state where I could no longer even do basic necessities for myself.

My blood pressure was extremely low and I was still passing out even though I was lying down. Being an independent person I found it highly humiliating for someone else to have to take care of my basic needs. I lay short of breath with a body that was like jelly, with huge tear drops in my eyes just saying "Lord help me." I knew the Lord's closeness in such an amazing way it was almost like if I had reached out I would've touched him!

Throughout the two weeks I was in hospital I had twelve drips put through me, countless blood tests and many scans and X-Rays. I did feel overwhelmed at times and so desperately wanted my body to work properly again. One night near the end of my stay in hospital I asked the nurse if I could try going in a wheelchair to the bathroom. I was so desperate to be well. We didn't get very far because I fainted and toppled out of the chair. That poor nurse didn't know what was coming but she kindly broke my fall! Prayer that night was just sobbing in the Lord's arms knowing that he was holding me close and I didn't even need to speak.

I think the funniest part of being in hospital was the day that I had to have a small procedure done. Apparently when I came out of the anaesthetic I was talking gibberish and shouting "I love marshmallows" really loudly! At least it gave everyone something to laugh at. The Bible does say that laughter is good medicine!

I think that my main reason for going into hospital was for the Lord to show me that even though I was at my weakest I could still serve him. My body may not have worked but my mouth did. The Lord opened many doors for me to share him with fellow patients and staff. It still amazes me to think how the Lord could use me when I was both physically and emotionally so low.

In the middle of my hospital stay a visitor brought me a little notebook. To me it was like receiving the crown jewels! I wrote:

Days have passed - in fact eight days. Eight long days that have taken me on a journey that I never dreamt I'd be going on. Yet a path nevertheless that the Lord has brought me down that has filled me with so much fight and hope, a path that has refreshed my soul because after months of isolation at home I've been among so many people and it's been so good to have company. I'm determined that I'm going to overcome this so that God can use all that I've been through to help someone else. A friend left me in a daily devotional called "Inspiring women" (Jan/Feb 2008). The Lord's really used it to speak to me.

"But God will redeem my life from the grave." Psalm 49:15 (NIV) "But God shows a signal, a total reversal of some situation. But God is a reminder that God is our redeemer and buys back those who put their trust in him." Also *"But God will shoot them with arrows... and bring them to ruin."* Psalm 64:7-8 (NIV). I believe God is going to shoot down with arrows this old illness that has invaded my body. He's going to rescue me!

Philippians 3:8 also spoke to me. *"But what things were gain to me, those I counted loss for Christ. Yea doubtless, and I count all things but loss for the excellency of the knowledge of Christ Jesus my Lord: for whom I have suffered the loss of all things, and do count them but dung, that I may win Christ."*

Truly there is nothing more important than knowing my Lord. I may have suffered the loss of physical capabilities but I've gained a deeper walk with him and that's priceless.

My Lord yet will I praise you. You are the Lord who heals, you are the Lord my healer and great and wonderful things you have done for me. You've heard the agonising cries of my heart every time I cried to you. Thank you that you care about even the tiny details of my life. Thank you for being with me on my nightmare day and getting me to hospital quickly. You've stood with me through every test and scan. Your strong hand of protection has covered me. Every needle, every blood test I've known you surrounding me. I'm overwhelmed with gratitude for every kind nurse and doctor and for every person who's visited me over the past days. You've knit my heart even more closely with each friend that you've blessed me with. Thank you for everyone's words of encouragement and life over me. At times there have been tears of joy at their words. You are an amazing God. Even though I'm still physically weak and I don't know when my bodies going to work properly again, my heart is totally in your hands.

I left hospital stable but no further forward. There's no medication or instant cure for ME. My mother cared for me until the glorious day came when I started to improve and could yet again see to my own needs! It was such a joy to be able to make a cup of tea for myself! I was rejoicing over being well enough to make that cup of tea after so long. I wasn't healed but thankfully I wasn't in a place of total physical oblivion anymore.

The best way to describe me when I couldn't get up was that I was like a ragdoll. I've written a poem about that ragdoll feeling. I hope it encourages any of you reading this who feels the same way that I did. The last line of the last verse is taken from Mark 5:41.

RAGDOLL

Ragdoll. Beautiful ragdoll. So carefully stitched and sewn.
Your constant companion who loved you so, no longer needs you
    for she's married and grown.
There you sit in that dark corner, forgotten and so alone.
You think your best days have come and gone. "It's over for me"
    you cry. "Into the attic I've been thrown."

Your memories transport you to a place far away.
Your girl took you everywhere. Laughter, joy, colour and fun packed
    every single day.
You felt useful, loved and important. You were the one who cushioned
    her tears when her day had been so grey.
No matter what storms raged outside, secure and content you were
    as in her arms you lay.

Everything's changed around you but you still look the same.
A permanent smile on your face. Blue eyes, blonde hair and Pollyanna's
    still your name.
Your soft body's lifeless, you look so helpless. Life for you has lost
    its sparkle, its ultimate aim.
Oh don't lose your fight Pollyanna! Let hope burn within you and set
    your dreams aflame.

Voices, noise, clattering. Oh what's going on? What's that stream of light?

You're being lifted. Your dreams are about to come true! Oh now
they're within your sight.
Another girl now holds you. You're her treasure, her delight.
Blessing has come. Your nightmare is over. Laughter and joy replace fear.
Your future is very bright.

I know how you felt dear ragdoll, because I'm now dwelling in my
personal attic.
My body is lifeless, weak, fragile and frail. Oh I'm tired of being sick.
I understand you losing your aim and sparkle. For I too feel like I'm
up against a wall of brick.
Yet deep down hope is surfacing. Even though I'm hard hit, to this
battle I will stick.

My Lord knit me together in the womb. He knows what's in store for
me for he is so wise.
He'll make a way. He'll bring me to a place of laughter, joy, blessing
and blue skies.
I'm looking to him for he's my all, my love, my prize.
I'll be no more a ragdoll when he takes my hand someday soon and says
"Damsel, I say unto thee, arise."

At the close of this chapter I just want to leave you with one more verse that
helped me at this time. No matter what you're going through don't give
up! You are going to make it! *"He delivereth and rescueth, and he worketh
signs and wonders in heaven and earth, who hath delivered Daniel from the
power of the lions."* Daniel 6:27

**"Setbacks are just step ups for God to show what he is able to do.
Funerals are for people who have accepted the thought that everything
is over. Don't do that! Instead tell the enemy I'm not dead yet."**

T.D. Jakes

CHAPTER 6
MEDICINE TO MY SOUL

My yo-yo like body gave me another good spell which I am truly thankful for! Yet it wasn't long until I found myself sliding down another snake and found myself at the bottom of the snakes and ladders board again. Coping with loneliness and being housebound has been my greatest struggle over the years of this illness. I've always loved being among people and really don't like excessive isolation at all! I developed a coping strategy one night as I lay studying my Bible, (I've added bits and pieces to this as I've rewritten it).

"Wherein the king granted the Jews which were in every city to gather themselves together, and to STAND FOR THEIR LIFE, to destroy, to slay, and to cause to perish, all the power of the people and province that would assault them."
Esther 8:11

Also. *"The Jews had light, and gladness, and joy, and honour. And in every province, and in every city, whithersoever the king's commandment and his decree came, the Jews had joy and gladness, a feast and a good day. And many of the people of the land became Jews; for the fear of the Jews fell upon them."*
Esther 8:16-17

This is an amazing passage. It's so profound and full of hope. The first thing that the Lord is saying to me tonight is: "Joanne, stand for your life." All I have to do is keep standing firm for my king. He sees the power of the enemy over me to assault me, to discourage me and to cause me to give up hope. My question is: What does it really mean to stand for my life? How, when I'm so physically weak that my dreams are dying before my eyes? In this passage standing firm meant that the Jews had to take action, they had to go out and fight. They had to slaughter everyone who longed to kill them. In other words they had to kill the root of the problem. The NIV puts it: *"The king's edict granted the Jews in every city the right to assemble and PROTECT THEMSELVES."* Esther 8:11

What action can I take when action is out of the question physically? What action can I take to protect myself emotionally and mentally when I'm physically awful?

1 **By not drowning in my own troubles. Stay focused on others needs and do all I can to help.**

"A kind-hearted woman gains respect ... a kind man benefits himself."
Proverbs 11:16-17 (NIV)

I can still lift the phone and write cards. Being housebound is no excuse to withdraw into my shell and close others out. Tiredness isn't an excuse to be dry with people and not put in any effort. I used to have a poem on my bedroom wall that's always challenged me so much.

IT'S NOT ALWAYS EASY

It's not always easy to smile and be nice,
  when we are called to sacrifice.
It's not always easy to put others first,
  especially when tired and feeling our worst.
It's not always easy to do the Fathers will.
  It wasn't so easy to climb Calvary's hill.
But we as his children should learn to obey.
  Not seeking our own but seeking his way.
It's not always easy to fight the good fight.
  But it's always good and it's always right.

By Glenda Fulton Davies.

It really is a challenge to put others first when tired and at our worst but by the grace of God it's do-able. This quote that I came across the other day really fits in here too!

"If I can stop one heart from breaking. I shall not live in vain. If I can ease one life the aching or cool one pain. Or help one fainting robin into his nest again. I shall not live in vain."

Emily Dickinson

2 **By daily trying to see the good in every situation that I'm in and to keep a thankful heart.**

"He that diligently seeketh good procureth favour." (Proverbs 11:27) Also *"A merry heart maketh a cheerful countenance: but by sorrow of the heart the spirit is broken."* Proverbs 15:13

There are so many things that I can praise my God for daily. It's not all doom and gloom. The Lord has blessed me so much in spite of me not being able to get out of bed at the minute. For a start I am still his and he is mine! Illness can't change that. I can praise him for family, friends, hundreds of people praying for me and people's kindness! Even simple things like warmth, shelter, pyjamas, nice food, CD's to listen to and cups of tea.

Psalm 150:6 urges, *"Let every thing that hath breath praise the Lord."* That's me. I still have breath in my lungs and as long as I've got air in my lungs I have every reason to praise God for his goodness to me. I don't want to rob God of his glory by withholding my praise from him.

3 Watch my speech.

While it's good to open up to people and not bottle everything up, it's still so important to keep my speech full of hope even when feelings scream the opposite. Proverbs 12:14 says *"A man shall be satisfied with good by the fruit of his mouth..."* Also Proverbs 16:24 *"Pleasant words are as an honeycomb, sweet to the soul, and health to the bones."*

I can't choose my situation but I can choose the words that come out of my mouth. According to Solomon pleasant words are health to the bones. I don't want to be in this situation a day longer than I need to be. I don't want to be like the Israelites who wound up in the desert longer than they needed to be because of their bad attitudes and complaining hearts. As I meditated on this I penned this little poem.

Lord let my words bless, not bring others stress.
Don't let me complain or moan and groan and be a pain.
Lord let me be a fountain clean so on you others will lean.
I don't want my waters to be both bitter and sweet.
Let them bring refreshing from the noon day heat.
If death and life are in the power of my tongue.
I choose life Lord, everyday till the battle is won.

4 Receive encouragement from others and hide it in my heart.

Every card that comes in the post and every word that every visitor speaks I want to fully digest. I never want to be too proud to admit to needing help. Proverbs 12:25 says: *"Heaviness in the heart of man maketh it stoop: but a good word maketh it glad."*

Also Proverbs 15:30 *"The light of the eyes rejoiceth the heart, and a good report maketh the bones fat."* Over the years of this illness people's encouragement has truly been medicine to my soul. It's been soul refreshing that just whenever I needed someone most that a visitor came. I wrote this one day after a couple of friends left.

MEDICINE TO MY SOUL

Today was dark, dreary, lonely and hard.
My body felt awfully weak. My spirit crushed and scarred.
An aching emptiness filled my heart for I felt like a useless lump of lard.
I prayed for help and then a car drove into our yard.

In the car were angels! Clad in jeans with smiley faces.
Laughter and joy filled my room as we travelled in our chat
 to many places.
Medicine to my soul! The laughter brought a sweet oasis,
Of shelter from the storm. O what hope my soul embraces.

What a beautiful time of refreshing I found.
Where my broken spirit with bandages was bound.
Without your help Lord I would have drowned.
O bless my jeans-clad angels and in your love let them abound."

All of you Angels and beautiful spirited encouragers, who are reading this, please keep doing what you are doing. You are priceless.

5 Learn to rest in God.

Proverbs 14:30 (NIV) says. *"A heart at peace gives life to the body..."* I truly need to just lie back and let the Lord fill me with his peace and stop fussing and fretting about what I can and can't do. I've mentioned already that over the months and years of this illness I've received a deeper walk with God. He is the best medicine to the soul available. I always made time for meaningful prayer times and Bible studies before I was ill. I came to know the Lord as saviour at a very young age when I was 6 or 7. The date and time have always been unclear to me and as a teenager I worried that maybe I wasn't really a Christian because I couldn't remember the date. Then I heard someone on UCB radio speaking from his heart. He said "I know I'm his because I know that there was a definite point where I confessed with my mouth the Lord Jesus and believed in my heart that God raised him from the dead and I am saved. I may have lost the birth certificate with specifics on it but I am his." The thought of having lost my spiritual birth certificate put my mind at ease. I remember so clearly at a children's meeting being told what Jesus had done for me. I knew heaven and hell were real places and I realised that without Jesus I would perish. I'd have no hope after death. I remember in my childlike way asking Jesus to forgive me, come into my heart and be my saviour. I may not know the exact date but I remember making my choice for Christ at that time. I didn't dare live or die without him. Down through the years as I've walked with him the Lord has shown me more and more of himself. When I was 15 years old I got baptised by immersion as I sign of my commitment to the Lord. I'll always remember the words of the chorus that was being sung as I went through the waters: "My heart will sing to you because of your great love. A love so rich so pure. A love beyond compare. The wilderness, the barren place become a blessing in the warmth of your embrace."

It wasn't until the past few years of trial and illness that I've fully grasped how the wilderness and the barren places can be a blessing in the Lord's embrace. This poem reflects some of my experiences with the Lord in the wilderness. Before reading this some may not know what I mean by a "Bethel." I simply mean a meeting place with God. Just like Jacob in the Bible called his meeting place with the Almighty "Bethel."

DIVINE SECRET PLACES

Dwelling in your divine secret place.
Hearing you call my name.
Connecting with you in sweet harmonious bliss.

Heartsick I am for you Lord who built my frame.

Dwelling here I stop my striving.
Here I no longer depend on me.
In this place I am your daughter.
Sitting contented on my father's knee.

Over the years I've had exhilarating Bethels.
My room, the fields, the beach and the swings!
Awesome Lord with power you descended.
Oh I soared high in you on dove's wings.

Then came the Bethels of holiness.
As I sat with the dying in worship and prayer.
Oh Holy ground where I sensed your heartbeat.
Breathing you into my spirit as the purest of air.

Knowing you in my sufferings has drawn me nearer to your heart.
This bed, the sofa, and the hospital.
Bethels where you've knit my spirit with yours in a bond that can't
   be torn apart.

I'm yours for service or sacrifice.
Let me humbly obey for you know best.
My flesh cries for service and activity.
For now you want me to be still, to abide,
   to feast on you as your invited guest.

I know I've only scratched the surface.
More Bethels is my plea. Draw me to you with loves strong cord.
My whole being screams out;
"My soul longeth, yea, even fainteth for your courts," dear Lord. Psalm 84:2

Knowing the Lord and resting in him makes coping so much easier.

6 Stay faithful to the Lord in every small way that I possibly can.

"Most men will proclaim every one his own goodness: but a faithful man who

can find." Proverbs 20:6. Also; "God has no greater ground for those who are unfaithful where they are." Elizabeth George

I can stay faithful to God in lots of little ways. Some already have been mentioned. I can stay faithful in prayer and Bible study, in attitudes, in giving, in trust and in displaying a quiet confidence in God. That was the end of my six points but my journal continued that night.

> Not only was the word of the Lord to me today to 'Stand for my life.' There was great hope in this passage in Esther. After the nightmare, the fear and the bloodshed came God's blessing. So too, I've got to believe that after I've done all I can to stand and when this nightmare of illness is over that:
>
> Joanne SHALL have *"joy and gladness, a feast and a good day."* Esther 8:17. Glory to his name! Night.

Come with me now as we meet some other people who've walked different paths of pain and are going to share something about what got them through darker days.

"Smooth seas do not make skilful sailors."

African Proverb

CHAPTER 7
OTHER PEOPLE'S EXPERIENCES

This chapter will take the form of a series of interviews. Let's first of all meet Esther (not her real name). Esther is a Christian lady who is happily married yet for years she has longed for a baby. Esther knows what it's like to dwell in the desert place of unfulfilled dreams.

Q1. *After marriage the greatest desire of your heart was to be a mother. How did you feel when you realised nothing was happening?*

"Growing up in a church environment I became involved in looking after the babies in crèche and taking a Sunday School class. It was at this time in my life that I fell in love with children. I hoped and longed for a baby but as the years went past nothing happened and a feeling of deep grief for the child I never had stepped in. It was a devastation type of feeling. However in the midst, knowing that God's ways are better than my ways kept me sane and does to this very day."

Q2. *I've heard people talk about how unfair it seems to couples who really want a child when they hear of all the unwanted teenage pregnancies. Did you ever feel that it was unfair? Can you describe your feeling of loss?*

"I can honestly say that although my human feelings surface (e.g. seeing and hearing of friends and family having children and me not having that joy and privilege) I just know that God is working in mine and my husbands lives, even though this childless path is not one we would've chosen. I don't think that my not having a baby is unfair though sometimes it's hard to understand why I didn't become a mum. When I reach that point of frustration that's when I have to keep trusting my God for his plans for us."

Q3. *How did you get through the blackness of this experience?*

"Not having a child of my own and seeing others experience that joy has naturally caused me to struggle with a whole concoction of emotions at different times in my life. I am always happy for the couple but it can be hard. I have four nephews and one niece and love them like my own so that's helped me so much. My sister and I laugh and say that she made up for the both of us. My mum has been and is a great support; she is always encouraging me to stay strong in the Lord and focus on and to live for him. God has blessed me with a loving husband, family and friends and has provided for all our needs and more."

Q4. *Was there a Bible verse, poem or hymn or all three that you held onto in the midst of pain? Or someone who inspired you?*

"The Bible verse that I hold onto through hard and difficult times is Isaiah 41:10; *"Fear thou not, for I am with thee: be not dismayed; for I am thy God: I will strengthen thee; yea I will help thee; yea, I will uphold thee with the right hand of my righteousness."*

"My dad was a great inspiration to me. My dad passed away about twelve years ago but he left me with many happy memories. He was ill from ever I was born; I knew him no other way. He had a kidney transplant which saw him through for thirty years. However my dad lost his sight, he never once saw what I looked like. My dad never felt sorry for himself. He prayed fervently for others and also with me at night. I saw first hand the blessings of peace and joy that God gave my father in the midst of pain so I've determined to follow in his footsteps."

Q5. *How did you reach the place of acceptance and contentment?*

"It was a slow climb to this place but an awesome assurance of my heavenly father's love for me and a deep assurance that no matter what happens in our lives God has it all worked out for his glory got me through. Life's not about having everything our own way and getting all our wants catered for. It's about yielding our lives totally to God and giving him all of us as our time here is so short. The words of the hymn; "Trust and obey for there's no other way to be happy in Jesus but to trust and obey" have always helped me gain perspective. I wrote this poem a long time ago when I was very discouraged about my situation. May it bless whoever reads it."

TRUSTING THE LORD

The only way forward is to trust the Lord,
When things go wrong, he will give you a song,

To fill your heart with hope and cheer.
Don't lose sight of his ways,
Trust his words they are Holy and dear.

But when we fret and hide away,
The gloom will conquer and ruin your day.
So hold your head high and lift your eyes upwards.
God made a rainbow just to say he loves us.

My friend is Christ, look upward and pray,
Thank the Lord for another new day,
A day that Christ has blessed for you,
Give thanks for small mercies for God will take care of you.

Esther has truly given God great glory in the way she's handled her unfulfilled dreams without becoming sour and full of blame towards God.

The next person that we are going to meet is Patricia Clarke from Coleraine. Patricia suffers from chronic illness. She is also paralysed completely from the waist down. Patricia has been in bed for thirteen years (without any seasons of brief reprieve like I get). Yet she is a true inspiration and is a channel of blessing. I've received countless cards from her over the years. She has a laptop and from her bed she orders lovely gifts for people to bless them.

This is a lady who is in total agony constantly and needs twenty five tablets for pain relief every day. Let's hear from her now.

Q1. *Briefly describe what your life was like before illness.*

"Busy, busy, busy getting on with daily things. I never ever thought about other people or them having problems or anyone being sick or poorly. My life was all good in every way. What a wake-up call I got."

Q2. *How did you cope when you were first diagnosed? What changes had to be made to your life? How did you feel?*

"Awful! What a terrible time. I was in shock. I just closed myself off from everyone, locked the door and took the phone off the hook. Everything had to change from getting myself washed to getting dressed. Carers came into my daily life to which I was not very happy. I felt that my life had been taken over and that I didn't have a choice in it. It all changes when choices are taken away from you and you have no control over it. What an awful time I had coming to terms with everything."

Q3. *What helps you to cope everyday? (You're always smiling and full of kindness!) Are there any blessings you've gained as a result of your suffering?*

"The Lord! From the time I open my eyes in the morning until I go to sleep at night he is always by my side. The Lord is so important to me. I couldn't get through a day without him being in my life. I knew the Lord before I became ill but never in the way I do now. Each day as I lie here I draw closer to him and put my full trust in him. Before illness I was always to busy to be with God and life felt so good. Now I pray for everyone and always think of others which I never did before. Before I was so selfish and now it has all changed for the good. I can say thank you Lord. I never used to smile much but now I smile a lot as the Lord took over and changed me. I am more happy and content in my spirit and if I can help anyone else I do."

Q4. *Has there been a Bible verse, poem or hymn that you've held onto in the midst of pain?*

"The hymn that was sung at John and I's wedding day had definitely taken on deeper meaning and brought me much comfort in adversity. That's Psalm 23; *"The Lord is my shepherd: I shall not want... he restoreth my soul... he leadeth me in the paths of righteousness... yea though I walk through the valley of the shadow of death, I will fear no evil: for thou art with me; thy rod and thy staff they comfort me.... Surely goodness and mercy shall follow me, all the days of my life and I will dwell in the house of the Lord forever."* These are words of life to me which have carried me through when I've felt like despairing."

Q5. *What has been the hardest part of having an illness over the years?*

"Coming to terms with it all. Even today I still fight that battle. I struggle at times with not being able to do what I want in life. I miss the simple everyday things that I used to enjoy like going shopping with my hubby or my daughter. Also losing me in it all. I still grieve for the life I had before in terms of physical strength. Though like I said before I have to keep focused on what's good in my life especially knowing God better. Also John is such an amazing husband and great friend. He cares for me so much and helps me every day. He is treasure in darkness."

The next person we're going to meet has been through the desert of grief. Janine lost her mother to cancer when she was just 19 years old and about to start university. Janine Clyde is also from Coleraine.

Q1. *You lost your mother at 19 just before you went off to university. What happened and could you describe how you felt at that time?*

"Mum began to feel unwell around mid-August. She had gone to see the doctor but had been misdiagnosed. She went into hospital as I was preparing for university, I remember filling out the halls accommodation forms and keeping her company at her bed-side. No one at this stage realised how serious it was. I moved into Queen's University's Elm's Village halls with the help of my dad and began to settle in. Mum had been moved from our local hospital to the Royal Victoria in Belfast so I was able to go across town and see her when I could. It still didn't seem that serious. In the morning of the day I was to register at Queen's I went to see mum and found my visit very upsetting. She was really unwell. I wanted to show her a new t-shirt that I had bought and I had come in expecting to cheer her up with stories of halls and my new neighbours but it became very clear that normal conversation was not on the cards that day. She was very out of it and in pain and not really aware that I was even there. I was in tears and the doctors said they were doing everything they could to make her comfortable. I thought at the time this was an odd way of putting it. They had discovered at this stage that she had cancer and it was terminal. They had told my dad but he had not managed to tell me yet. So off I went to get my picture taken for my student card at registration with my eyes all red yet in complete denial of what was happening and clinging to the belief that everything was eventually going to be ok. My brother was coming home from London the next day, having cancelled travel plans with his friends. He had caught from my dad's tone that something was terribly wrong but I could not believe that to be true – it wasn't an option in my head. So when Peter asked if mum was going to die, I was shocked by the question. I almost laughed but in the pause between the question and my dad's quiet 'yes,' panic grasped me. For the next few days I was in total denial and in just over a week we had lost her."

Q2. *How did you cope initially through those early days of loss? Was there any particular Bible verse, poem or hymn that you've held onto in the midst of your pain? Explain why it is special to you.*

"Initially I coped by avoiding the subject. I got angry over little things, annoyances that would barely have bothered me under normal circumstances. Someone used my mug for their tea and I almost exploded. It could seem almost silly looking back on it but the anger was so real at the time. I'm not sure if I have ever felt angrier. In those early days, in my darkest moments what I felt most keenly was isolation. I did not know anyone who had gone through this and I felt misunderstood by many. But I did not feel hopeless. For though my world was being turned upside down, and though the vision I had of my future lay in tatters at my feet I knew that my Heavenly Father held me in his hands. When you go through dark times you must hold on to what you know to be true in the light. I know that God knows the plans that he has for me and they are good. He has given me a hope and a future. But the verse that most powerfully affected me through this time was *'to live is Christ, and to die is gain.'* (Philippians 1:21) The reason this is so powerful for me is because it reminds me that death has been defeated, so not only do we do not have to worry about it but we can actually rejoice in life and in death because the one who saves us lives!"

Q3. *Is there any particular blessing that you've gained as a result of your suffering?*

"Absolutely, I was so blessed in the suffering. It was not in my own strength that I faced this personal crisis. It was in God's immeasurable abundance that I stood. The psalms proclaim that *'as the mountains are round about Jerusalem, so the Lord is round about his people from henceforth even forever.'* (Psalm 125:2) Through this time God was showing me what it truly means to rely on his strength because I could no longer rely on my own. He showed me how it was possible to experience joy despite circumstances. A friend of mine came over to comfort me and while we were talking and she was sympathising I suddenly realised we were talking about two different things. She saw death as the worst thing that could happen; she saw it as the end, a hopeless absence of life. But I knew different. I knew that the worst part of this was that I was missing my mum terribly but that she had gone on to be with her heavenly father. She had an audience with the King! So I rejoiced. I rejoiced that God had come to earth and reconciled us to himself. I rejoiced in the astonishing grace that brings us all into his presence and I praised God."

Q4. *Is there anything else that you would like to add?*

"There is a song by 'Casting Crowns' which asks 'if we are the body, why aren't His arms reaching?' The lyrics throughout the piece are embedded with the assumption that it is the role of the church to be Jesus to the world. This was what I experienced at this time. My family was surrounded with prayer and reaching arms, the support and comfort of God's people, and not only from our own church. I thank God for the people in my life that recognise the importance of prayer and the deep impact that it has; prayer changes things. So I would encourage you to underestimate neither this fact nor the importance of showing Christ's love to others. We are the body - so reach!"

The last person that we are going to meet is Linda McAuley from Ballymoney. Linda has severe MS. She is mostly housebound and depends on carers yet she is strong in God. Let's hear from her now.

Q1. *Briefly describe what your life was like before illness?*

"I lived a full life, I was very active, I was a homemaker, I walked my dog five miles per day, I helped on the farm, and I was very social. I shopped, I cooked, I baked. I was blessed with good health all my life. I was actually so busy with life that I'd put the Lord on the backburner, life was really good."

Q2. *How did you cope when you were diagnosed?*

"It took me a long time to accept that I had a debilitating illness. My heart was broken but I had to survive. I had to use my faith more than ever. At this time I held onto Psalm 27:14: *'Wait on the Lord: be of good courage, and he shall strengthen thine heart: wait, I say on the Lord.'"*

Q3. *What changes had to be made to your life? How did you feel?*

"A lot of changes happened in my life which were out of my control. I literally had been working, sleeping and eating in the daily grind pattern that we're all so familiar with so when I fell ill I had to make it through using my faith like never before. I had to learn to lean on God in a whole new dimension. *"The Lord upholdeth all that fall and raiseth up all those that be bowed down."* Psalm 145:14.

"I was overcome with feelings that I'd never felt before. I was scared. My future looked really bleak. I had to believe that I wasn't going to get any worse. I couldn't imagine a wheelchair. Fear gripped me until God spoke to me through 2 Timothy 1:7. *"For God hath not given us the spirit of fear; but of power... and of a sound mind."*

Q4. *What helps you cope each day?*

"I take one day at a time. I cope by resting secure in the knowledge that the Lord is in control. I know he is able to heal me though I just want his will for my life whatever that will is. I just want the Lord to use me in my wheelchair or out of it."

Q5. *Has there been a Bible verse, a poem or hymn that you've held onto in times of pain?*

"A verse came to me *"But for a season."* I've held onto this since I was diagnosed. I believe that my situation is just for a season. Deuteronomy 4:31 has also brought me great comfort; *"For the Lord thy God is a merciful God. He will not forsake thee...* Another verse that I quote to myself a lot when I'm overwhelmed is Philippians 4:13 *"I can do all things through Christ which strengtheneth me."* Another thought that comforts me is that most of the people in the Bible that God used mightily went through a breaking of some sort."

Q6. *What has been the hardest part of your having this illness?*

"I've found it hard to cope with losing my old life and old friends. I struggle with not being able to socialise like I used to because of the way that this illness has affected me. I've become very isolated because of the chronic fatigue that goes with MS. It's hard for healthy people to understand just how fatigue is because my appearance doesn't give anything away as I carefully put on make-up everyday and fix my hair. I know what it's like to put on a brave show in front of people but on the inside be totally exhausted. It's nothing like just healthy tiredness when you've done a days' work and need to go to bed it's constant. It's like a plug being pulled out and every ounce of strength that you have being continually sucked out of you. At times it is frustrating but the Lord has given me contentment from within and a deep sense of his peace."

Q7. *Is there anything else that you would like to add?*

"I am blessed by a great team of professionals, friends and family who make my life a bit easier. I'm blessed by a lovely comfortable home which is important when you're sick. I've met new people through this illness which I probably wouldn't have come across in my normal life. It has opened up a lot of things which I had no previous idea of understanding like taking time to think. I'm more reflective and thoughtful now.

"I believe that this is a learning curve. I'm learning how to be patient. I'm working really hard daily to keep my muscles strong if I can. I'm doing all the correct things I can, according to the professional team around me. I'm learning like I've said to wait upon the Lord."

These four people have all in spite of their hardships found myrtle trees in the midst of life's briars, they've found fir trees instead of thorns. I hope their examples will touch your lives and inspire in you courage to keep fighting.

I'd like to end this chapter with a poem that I've written.

IN SICKNESS AND IN HEALTH

In sickness and in health you've been everything to me.
When my spirit's felt crushed, your spirits brought me liberty.
When all I've seen are dead ends, you've heard each desperate plea.

When panic's engulfed me and my future's seemed a haze.
   You've focused my eyes on Calvary's tree.

Precious heavenly bridegroom, your love unlocks the door.
To lifting me up above the storm and causing me to soar.
What a bliss haven I've found close to your bosom.
   What a rich treasure store.
Thank you for your amazingness beloved Lord.
   You've blessed me to the core.

"Life breaks us all but many are made strong at the broken places."

Ernest Hemmingway

CHAPTER 8
TWO INSPIRING BIBLICAL MEN

As I've studied the Bible there have been many people whose examples have strengthened my faith as I've journeyed through. These are great examples of coping with adversity. Let's now look together at Paul and Stephen.

PAUL

Paul is a brilliant example of coping with affliction. I'm never going to cover every aspect of Paul's life and ministry as it's so huge but let's home in on some specific examples to encourage our hearts.

1 HE WASN'T A COMPLAINER, HE WAS CONTENT

"Paul had physical handicaps that most of us would have used as excuses for staying home, yet he evangelised the regions beyond. He endured 'troubles, hardships and distresses... beatings, imprisonments and riots... hard work, sleepless nights and hunger' but didn't complain about it. He had a thorn in his flesh, 'a messenger of Satan' that tormented him, yet he kept on going. 'My grace is sufficient for you' the Lord told him."[6]

It's hard to believe that instead of complaining Paul said; Philippians 4:11-12 *"...For I have learned, in whatsoever state I am, therewith to be content. I know both how to be abased, and I know how to abound: everywhere and in all things I am instructed both to be full and to be hungry, both to abound and to suffer need."*

Paul could honestly say he had learnt the secret of contentment with outward circumstances, whether he had little or much. He knew his Lord would not fail to give him what was necessary and to strengthen him to face every situation. The word translated 'content' means self-sufficient. It was regarded by the Stoics as high virtue to be detached from outward circumstances and to have resources in oneself to meet every situation. Paul uses the word in the sense of being independent of circumstances, but his all sufficient resources were he said "Through him who gives me strength." The living Lord Jesus.[7]

As I face future days of recovery this is exactly the place I want to remain in. A place of contentment. I strive and get impatient, Paul didn't! What a wonderful example to look up to.

2 PAUL HAD A NO SURRENDER SPIRIT

In Acts 14:19-20 Paul was left for dead. *"And there came thither certain Jews from Antioch and Iconium who persuaded the people, and, having stoned Paul, drew him out of the city, supposing he was dead."*

Paul simply 'rose up' and continued to preach despite what had happened to him. He even returned to Lystra and Iconium the places where he'd been stoned and left for dead. *"Confirming the souls of the disciples, and exhorting them to continue in faith, and that we must through much tribulation enter into the kingdom of God."* Acts 14:22. He didn't lick his wounds and give up at the first sign of trouble he triumphed over it so he could continue spreading the good news. Paul had received a heavenly calling on the Damascus road and he didn't let his feelings or any other circumstance keep him from fulfilling it. Acts 26:18 sums up his calling well; *"To open their eyes and to turn them from darkness to light and from the power of Satan unto God, that they may receive forgiveness of sins, and inheritance among them which are sanctified by faith that is in me."*

He was devoted to his saviour and willing to obey him no matter what the cost. There's an awful lot of preaching going about today that pictures coming to Jesus as a bed of roses. It promises health, wealth and prosperity. Paul knew that being a Christian didn't exempt him from tough times, after all his saviour had borne a cross so why shouldn't he have to? He ploughed on and didn't get off the bus at the first sign of trouble.

3 PAUL SANG IN HIS PRISON CELL

I love to sing. Many of us love to sing. Singing is an expression of a happy heart. We all know that it's easy to sing and praise God when everything's rosy but do we sing when the harsh bitter winds of pain are howling at our hearts door? Acts 16:25 says; *"And at midnight Paul and Silas prayed, and sang praises unto God: and the prisoners heard them."* Wow! Singing in their darkest hour! "It takes grace to sing to the Lord from the heart. It took grace for David to sing to the Lord in those Psalms. It took grace for Jesus to sing a hymn and go out and die on a cross. It took grace for Paul and Silas to sing hymns in the Philippian prison."[8]

To think that Jesus sang when he knew the exact details of the horrific death that he was going to die really amazes and humbles me. The easiest reaction is always a doom and gloom sense of dismal foreboding but the hardest reaction brings great blessing.

"The picture of Paul and Silas praying and singing hymns while clamped in stocks in their damp dark cell is an enduring one. Little wonder the other prisoners were listening to them: whether they were regarded as holy men or just lunatics, no one could accuse them of being dull. It's unlikely that Paul and Silas were praying for their release since they didn't make use of it when offered (Acts 16:28,37). The other prisoners could hardly fail to have regarded the violent earthquake that threw all the prison doors open and loosened everybody's chains as a supernatural answer to Paul and Silas' midnight session."[9]

Their singing praises even in darkness brought breakthrough and loosed chains that bound them. It's only speculation on my part but I think Paul and Silas may have prayed for God to use their dark experience for his glory even unto the salvation of souls. After all, through it all he was able to stop the jailor committing suicide and he led him and his family to Jesus and baptized them.

4 PAUL HAD AN UNSHAKEABLE TRUST IN GOD

In Acts 27 Paul was in the midst of a 'could be' tragedy. Paul was on a voyage to Rome. "From the beginning of the sea part of the voyage the 'winds were against the boat and it made slow headway' and moved along the coast with difficulty. In Acts 27:13-20 a gentle south wind quickly turned into a wind of hurricane force. This forced the crew to abandon control of their boat. The various precautions taken such as using cables to reinforce the ship's hull, lowering the sea anchor, throwing some of the cargo overboard and later even jettisoning part of the ship's tackle were the correct procedures."[10] Yet despite their efforts verse 20 says; *"And when neither sun nor stars in many days appeared, and no small tempest lay on us, all hope that we should be saved was then taken away."* An angel of God had appeared to Paul and assured him that nobody on the ship would lose their lives. Even though circumstances were screaming the opposite of what God had said Paul firmly believed it. He was so confident of it that he declared; *"Wherefore, sirs, be of good cheer: for I believe God, that it shall be even as (he) told me."* Acts 27:25

God did exactly as he said he would do, no harm came to anyone. After being shipwrecked on an Island called Melita for a short time they made it to Rome safely. That verse challenged me so much to cling to what God's promises through his word and even when things seem to be getting worse instead of better I need to keep reminding myself to be of good cheer for it shall be even as he told me.

5 PAUL LEFT A LEGACY OF TEACHING AND ENCOURAGEMENT FROM HIS PRISON CELL

I wonder had Paul not been in chains would we have such a wealth of encouragement left for us? Paul suffered proactively. While he still had breathe in his lungs he preached, handled church problems and encouraged all those in the new churches he'd founded to keep going and stay strong in faith. He could've sat in his cell and got himself worked up to such a state of distress that he might've closed the outside world off and focused on his own misery but he didn't. His heart was always full of compassion for the needs of others even when his own life wasn't going so well. It was Paul who penned the inspiring words in 2 Corinthians 1:4-5 *"Who comforteth us in all our tribulation, that we may be able to comfort them which are in any trouble, by the comfort wherewith we ourselves are comforted of God. For as the sufferings of Christ abound in us, so our consolation also aboundeth by Christ."*

Paul encourages his readers by pointing out that while his ministry may have been attended by many troubles it made it possible to share in God's comfort and pour that comfort out to others. Paul had found a strengthening grace in the midst of pain and like a fountain spring he poured out all that God poured in. His situation was far from hopeless because he was using it all for God's glory. Paul dared to be outward looking instead of inward looking.

Through all Paul's experiences and through his legacy one thing is very clear to me. God does not waste our time, He will use our past and present so we may serve him with our futures. Paul co-operated with the Lord through every trial by placing his hands in the Lord's. God wasted nothing and used everything that Paul had put at his disposal.

STEPHEN

In our part of the world today no one gets martyred simply for being a Christian. Even though this is something that we don't experience I believe Stephen's reaction to his suffering and how God used it for good are nuggets of pure gold for us to look at and learn from.

"The name 'Stephen' comes from the Greek word *stephanos* which means a 'victor's crown,' the crown that the winning athletes received at the Greek Olympics... Stephen received a crown in heaven, but he also earned a crown on earth. How? By being faithful to use his gifts and opportunities so that the Lord could "promote" him to new ministries."[11] Stephen is named among the seven men who were called to be the church's first deacons. These deacons were to take care of practical matters that arose like food distribution among the widows. The word deacon simply means 'servant'. Stephen is introduced in Acts 6:5 as *"Stephen, a man full of faith and of the Holy Ghost."* "Stephen was a remarkably gifted man - he even did miracles (Acts 6:8) and yet he was happy to serve tables. His humility and faithfulness helped build his character and prepare him for greater things."[12] In Acts chapter 7 we see how Stephen was also a preacher. Stephen's listeners treated him exactly the same way that Jesus was treated, paying false witnesses and making accusations. His listeners hardened their hearts against him and against the truth that he presented and this led to his arrest and a trial before the religious leaders.

"To spare himself, all he had to do was deliver a compromising, placating speech. But he would rather die than betray his sacred trust. Admire his courage!"[13]

1 STEPHEN LOOKED UP: Acts 7:55

Stephen's speech was interrupted by the fury of his audience who 'gnashed their teeth at him' almost snarling in their anger and frustration. What would I have done if I'd been Stephen? Would I have had the strength to look heavenward or would I have sat paralysed and dazzled like a rabbit caught in the headlights? How often does our focus stay on the things that have hurt us, the suffering, the pain, the nightmare circumstances and the faces of the bullies that we meet in life?

A little girl called Susie was due to read out her poem in English class at school. This was something that the teacher encouraged her students to do often and it went towards their end of term grade. Every time Susie had got up in the past she'd stood dazzled, staring into the faces of her teacher and classmates. While every passing moment of her stuttering and trying to speak was ticking away her classmates would get restless and start to giggle. This time Susie asked her grandfather what she should do as she was sick with worry. Her grandfather told her simply 'Just look up.' "Look beyond the faces and picture the beautiful face of Jesus smiling at you. Don't look around you. Look up." Susie succeeded marvellously at reading out her poem. She started out nervously but she confidently remembered that Jesus was right there with her, smiling at her! Stephen didn't place his focus on the angry faces he looked up, right in the midst of his nightmare circumstance and something glorious happened. He saw *"The glory of God, and Jesus standing on the right hand of God."* Acts 7:55

"Stephen was granted a vision, which like the opening of heaven and the voice of God at Jesus's baptism and transfiguration, was not only meant to give him courage for the task ahead, but was also God's endorsement for the crucial change that was taking place."[14]

Stephen got an awesome vision of God in the midst of the pain simply because he chose to look up. He got his focus in the right place. Through all our sufferings if we like Stephen will simply look up we'll gain a deeper walk with God and see him more clearly. It's not easy to look up, it's easier to dwell on what's around me but with God's help I'm determined to keep looking up.

2 HE BECAME LIKE JESUS IN HIS SUFFERINGS

While Stephen was looking up the mob: "Covered their ears and yelled out so as not to hear anymore of the supposed blasphemy. The mob was unable to wait for the niceties of a trial and without officially pronouncing a verdict of sentence they dragged him out of the city and began to stone him."[15]

Stephen echoed the heart of Jesus in his responses to his unfair treatment. *"And they stoned Stephen, calling upon God, and saying, Lord Jesus receive my spirit."* (Acts 7:59) Jesus while he hung on the cross had prayed *"Father, into thy hands I commend my spirit."* Luke 23:46

Stephen committed himself totally to God's hands trusting him to the very end even when everything was going against him. I used to know a little boy who when he had learned to crawl kept putting himself in danger's path by constantly heading to the door. Someone could've easily opened the door and hurt him but every time we lifted him away from the door he went straight there again. He was restless in my hands because I stopped him from getting his own way. As a little child he couldn't understand that I needed him to trust me to keep him away from danger. He didn't understand my reasons but I was actually working in his favour. Stephen didn't strive against God, he threw himself into God's arms and knew that no matter how it looked God was working in his favour.

In Acts 7:60 he also prayed; *"Lord lay not this sin to their charge."* Again he echoed Jesus who had prayed: *"Father, forgive them: for they know not what they do."* Luke 23:34

Stephen chose to forgive. By forgiving the people his circumstance wasn't changed but his own heart was set at liberty. Stephen chose his attitude when he could choose nothing else. Matthew 5:8 says; *"Blessed are the pure in heart: for they will see God."* By forgiving his oppressors he kept himself beautifully pure before God. That's how he reacted to suffering. Maybe your situation of heart crushing agony has been caused by somebody else and you're living daily with the voice of your accuser before you as you churn what happened over and over again in your mind. Choose not to get caught up in the 'Blame game' forgive whoever's wronged you and release them to God by praying for them. You'll not instantly get out of your circumstance but God will draw near to his pure hearted child who chooses to rise above 'smouldering anger' and he'll bless you abundantly for it. I remember reading a simple question years ago that said "Are you a victim or a victor?" I want to be a victor like Stephen.

3 THE BIGGER PICTURE.
WHAT STEPHEN'S SUFFERING ACCOMPLISED

"Stephen had so much to live for, and we wonder why God permitted him to be killed. But his prayer and the witness of his life accomplished more than most people's lives. For Stephen, his death meant coronation and he received his crown. Stephen gave an unforgettable demonstration of Christ like love for his accusers and his murderers, and this must've deeply affected Saul the persecutor who was standing there. Years later he mentioned Stephen's death to the Lord. (Acts 22:20) It was one of the goads that God used to convict Saul of his need for a Saviour."[16] Acts 26:14

Wow! To think that Stephen's death was one of Paul's first pointers to Christ. Like we've just looked at, Paul was an awesome soul winner, church planter and he left a legacy of inspiration through his writings. God was working out his plan even when it seemed like he was doing nothing.

What did Stephens's death do for the church in Jerusalem? "It led to greater persecution so that the saints were scattered like seeds, and wherever they landed they produced fruit, Acts 8:1-4, 11:19-21."[17] More people came to know Jesus as Saviour as a result of Stephen's death.

Even though you don't understand the ins and outs of what you're going through, take heart from Stephen and his legacy. Maybe you think that you're doing very little for God because of your limitations but maybe one of your kindly acts in the midst of your pain will go further than you think. Maybe someone will be so inspired by your witness that they'll turn to Christ. Maybe that person will become a modern day Paul and accomplish things for God that you never dreamt possible. The small choices Stephen had by his actions certainly made a massive difference. God hasn't changed and he's still working out his will in awesome ways!

"Our brokenness is the wound through which the full power of God can penetrate our beings and transfigure us in him."

Author unknown

CHAPTER 9
BIBLICAL WOMEN OF FAITH

RUTH & NAOMI

As I've read and studied though the book of Ruth something beautiful kept coming to my mind. It's this; "Life can rob you of everything except your character if you choose to let nothing touch it."

In Ruth 3:11 (NIV) Boaz said of Ruth; *"You are a woman of noble character."* Life didn't rob Ruth of her Character so let's learn from her example!

When we first meet Ruth and Naomi it looked like everything had fallen apart for them and that things couldn't get much worse. The book opens in chapter 1 with three funerals. Naomi's husband, 'Elimelech' had died then after a while Ruth and Orphah's husbands Mahlon and Chilion also died. These three widows were left destitute. Verse 6 struck me; *"Then she (Naomi) arose with her daughters-in-law, that she might return from the country of Moab: for she had heard in the country of Moab how that the Lord had visited his people in giving them bread."*

Naomi must've been in agony of soul. They'd come to Moab because of a famine. "Their residence in Moab, meant to be temporary, lasted ten years and at the end of it Naomi was bereft both of a means of livelihood and of hope for the future."[18] However.

1 THEIR FEELINGS DIDN'T DICTATE THEIR DECISIONS

They arose. Losing someone we love is a soul crushing event. It's natural and good to cry and feel devastation and heartache. However, sometimes the loss of someone can lead to a paralysing sense of self-pity. If self-pity creeps in anger and bitterness will move in too. Naomi grieved but she didn't stagnate and give up on life. She made a decision. A decision to care for what remained in her life. She and her two daughters-in-law would die of starvation by just staying in the same place. Sometimes grief can paralyse people to the point that they no longer see any good in their lives.

Naomi firmly believed that God would take care of her. Naomi did bethink herself and urge her daughters in law to return to their families so that they would have the chance of marrying again. Again this shows that Naomi remained considerate, loving and kind to others even though her heart must've been aching and it would've been easier for her to demand that they come with her on her journey to bring her comfort. She chose to be selfless and not self-centred. I don't know if I'd have done the same thing if I'd been in her shoes by choosing to let go of the only people I had left in order to release them to a more comfortable life. Yes, in verse 20 Naomi said; *"Call me not Naomi; call me Mara: for the Almighty hath dealt very bitterly with me."* Even though Naomi initially felt bitter in her spirit her feelings did not dictate her decisions and eventually because of her determination to press through she was brought to a place of blessing again. That's what we find the women of the land declaring in Ruth 4:14-15; *"And the women said unto Naomi, Blessed be the Lord, which hath not left thee this day without a kinsman, that his name may be famous in Israel? And he shall be unto thee a restorer of thy life and a nourisher of thine old age, for thy daughter in law, which loveth thee, which is better to thee than seven sons hath borne him."*

Naomi got to be an ancestor of our Precious Lord Jesus. She arose and God blessed her!

2 FAITH GROWS IN THE HEAT

Naomi may have been thinking of Ruth and Orpah's welfare physically when she urged them to go back though she wasn't thinking of their spiritual needs by sending them back to pagan gods. Yet despite Naomi's shortcomings Ruth says: *"Thy people shall be my people and thy God my God."* (Ruth 1:16) Orpah went home but Ruth clung to her mother in law because Ruth had come to trust in the true and living God.

"When we consider Ruth's situation, it's really remarkable that she should come to have such a strong faith in God. She was living in a Jewish family that evidenced little faith in the God they professed to serve. After all, when famine came, they fled Bethlehem and went to get help in enemy territory. Couldn't they trust their God? And what kind of God allows three men to die and leave three widows almost helpless in the world?.. In spite of all this painful negative influence, by the grace of God, Ruth became a believer."[19]

Ruth in total commitment put care of Naomi before her own interests. Love is not self-seeking 1 Corinthians 13:4-5. Ruth was leaving her homeland, leaving her parents that were still living and settling among strangers even though she had no certainty that she would find acceptance. As I thought about this I realised that our pain can be a catalyst for change in our walks with God. As I've journeyed through this valley of illness I've found this to be true as I've grown stronger in God in the furnace. I'd loved and served him before my valley but the Lord has taken something apparently bad and used it for good! See Genesis 50.

Ruth's pain became a blessing in that she embraced the Lord wholeheartedly. Let's follow in her footsteps by doing likewise. Let's not get ourselves down by continually asking why or turning our backs on the one we need most. Walk him through every painful emotion and burden in prayer and he will draw near to the broken-hearted!

3 RUTH CHOSE TO MAKE THE MOST OF A BAD SITUATION

"Ruth and Naomi's immediate need was food. It was humiliating to be reduced to such poverty but because it was harvest time there was a means of self help. God's law stipulated that farmers were not to harvest the corners of their fields, but leave grain for the poor to collect."[20] Leviticus 19:9, 23:22.

After all Psalm 146:9 says; *"The Lord watches over the alien and sustains the fatherless and the widow."* Ruth decided to take advantage of this provision, but guessed that not all farmers would welcome people foraging on their land especially a foreigner. Though she knew nothing about any near relatives of her father-in-law she 'happened' to choose to glean in a field belonging to Boaz who was from the *clan of Elimelech.* Her choice of field was no accident; God had been her unseen guide."

"Had Ruth sat home mourning and complaining she never would have met Boaz and become his wife... You can't steer a car when the gears are in neutral. Get busy helping others, and the Lord will guide you... Ruth's work was not only difficult, but it was also somewhat humiliating, for in gleaning she was declaring her poverty and helplessness. Gleaners were people who lived on leftovers, but she didn't care. She was living in the Most Holy Place, under the wings of Jehovah, and he was working on her behalf."[21]

Ruth didn't mind humbling herself to do the lowliest of tasks if it meant putting food on the table and caring for her mother-in-law. Ruth certainly made the best of a bad situation in her motivation to care for Naomi even though she was still grieving the loss of her own husband. Sometimes (like we've talked about earlier in this book) we just have to lift the focus off ourselves when we're in pain and place it on God and others. Ruth was blessed abundantly. We all love the end of the story (especially if you're a romantic like me!) when Ruth married Boaz and how she got her name in the Messiah's genealogy. We all love happy endings but I hope like me you'll find treasure and strength in the examples of Naomi and Ruth as they triumphed over trouble before blessing came. I'll end where I began. Life never robbed Ruth of her character and it can't rob you either!

The final Bible character I'd like us to look at together is Hannah.

HANNAH

"The name Hannah comes from the Hebrew word that means 'grace' or 'favour'... Hannah was barren, and her husband's second wife Peninnah never let her forget it."[22] In 1 Samuel 1:8 we see that Hannah had no appetite; *"Then said Elkanah her husband to her, why weepest thou? And why eatest thou not and why is thy heart grieved? Am I not better to thee than ten sons?"*

When emotional turmoil hits people's lives often the first thing affected is their appetites. Some people feel like life has spun so badly out of control that they stop eating as it's the last thing they feel that they have control over. Of course this makes things worse as lack of food increases tiredness, inability to think straight and adds to depression. Still others react to circumstances by overindulging or 'comfort eating.' This again makes the situation worse as it results in feelings of guilt, failure and inadequacy. Hannah was so distressed that food was the last thing on her mind. This may have been Hannah's initial reaction but she had a strong faith in God.

1 HANNAH TOOK HER PAIN TO GOD

She didn't stay in a place of despair she took action. Verse 9 says 'She arose.'

Just like Naomi did. Verse 10 struck me; *"And she was in bitterness of soul, and prayed unto the Lord, and wept sore."* What this verse doesn't say is: She was in bitterness of soul and complained and moaned to her husband in a pity party way saying woe is me! It doesn't say that she reacted by gossiping about her husband's other nasty wife or lashing out at her when provoked. It doesn't say that she became angry at God for not giving her what she wanted and by hardening her heart to him. However, it does say *"She prayed unto the Lord and wept sore."* She looked to God in simple faith; she took her eyes off her circumstances and her feelings. Hannah chose to look beyond herself to the one who cares about our deepest needs. She also 'wept' like a child in God's arms. Some people think that crying is a sign of weakness but Hannah chose the better part. She released all her bottled up emotions to God and totally emptied herself with a childlike heart.

Up to this point Hannah really had endured so much. "Barrenness can still cause psychological distress, but it was much worse in OT times, in a culture where it was viewed as a disgrace for a married woman to have no children. Despite Elkanah's attempts to help and console Hannah, the unkindness of her rival wife Peninnah made her position intolerable."[23]

Each of us may face times of barrenness when nothing comes to pass in our work, service, and relationships. It's difficult to pray in faith when we feel so ineffective but as Hannah discovered prayer opens the way for God to work.

"The text calls Peninnah, Hannah's 'rival,' (1 Samuel 1:6-7) a Hebrew word that is related to words like *distress, anguish, enemy* and *hostility.* When we examine the words that describe Peninnah's attitudes and actions we can easily see that Hannah didn't have an easy time in her own house. Peninnah provoked and irritated until Hannah was bitter in her soul and could only weep. 'I am a woman who is deeply troubled,' she told Eli for she was in great 'anguish and grief.' Imagine living with that kind of emotional pressure day after day."[24]

The Peninnah's in our lives wear us down emotionally and spiritually. If you have someone in your life that is constantly negative, criticises constantly, who nitpicks and leaves you feeling drained and worthless, take the whole situation to God. Seek him for breakthrough in your situation and even if it takes a while in coming, keep tracing the rainbow through the rain until it does happen. Maybe your Peninnah is a marriage partner? Maybe a work colleague or friend? Keep pouring out your heart to God, don't harden it!

2 HANNAH'S PRAYING WAS SELFLESS AND HER MOTIVES WERE PURE

Hannah's prayer, 1 Samuel 1:11; *"And she vowed a vow, and said, O Lord of hosts, if thou wilt indeed look on the affliction of thine handmaid, and remember me, and not forget thine handmaid, but wilt give unto thine handmaid a man child, then I will give him unto the Lord all the days of his life, and there shall no razor come upon his head."*

"Be careful what you promise in prayer because God may take you up on it. Hannah so desperately wanted a child that she was willing to strike a bargain with God. God took her up on her promise and to Hannah's credit she did her part even though it was painful. (1 Samuel 1:27,28) ...When you pray, ask yourself, Will I follow through on any promises I make to God if he grants my request? It is dishonest and dangerous to ignore a promise, especially to God. God keeps his promises, and he expects you to keep yours."[25]

"The God-given son would be consecrated to God from birth to death. Numbers 6 describes how Israelites could voluntarily consecrate themselves to God's service for a fixed period of time. Such people where known as Nazirites, and they vowed never to cut their hair, a visible symbol of their dedication to God. In the same way, Hannah promised that her son would be a permanent Nazirite."[26]

This struck me. Even though Hannah was in agony of soul she was still alert to the low spiritual state of the nation and prayed that God would use their special son to bring Israel back to him. What an incredible sacrifice! Every mother wants to see their child grow up. They want to delight in every stage of their child's life. Like their first steps, first words, watching them play and watching them mature and marry. Hannah gave up her rights to all of this even in her pain because she cared about others spiritual states and lived to glorify God. Hannah wanted everyone to have an opportunity to know the God that she loved. The God that's our only hope. After praying Hannah: *"Went her way, and did eat and her countenance was no more sad."* 1 Samuel 1:18

3 HANNAH RESPONDED TO HER SITUATION WITH A HEART OF PRAISE

Even before Hannah's prayer was answered: verse 19; *"And they rose up in the morning early and worshipped before the Lord..."* Hannah still didn't have her answer. Yes, she had poured out her bottled up soul to God. Yes she'd received encouragement from Eli but at this stage she still didn't know if God had said yes or no. Even in her barrenness she could still worship her God. Hannah's example in continuing to worship God in the barren places and difficult hardships of life is one we must follow if we truly want to rise above our circumstances and have victory over them.

Yes, Hannah's prayer was answered and she gave birth to a baby boy called 'Samuel.' Plus later the Lord rewarded her pure motives and sacrifice and not only gave her one son but; *"The Lord visited Hannah, so that she conceived, and bare three sons and two daughters. And the child Samuel grew before the Lord."* 1 Samuel 2:21.

However, the main point of this chapter is to show how these Bible characters reacted in the midst of suffering. "The story of Hannah should not be read as a promise that God will always remove barrenness or any other physical problem though it does underline the value of believing prayer. Its chief purpose is to show how God overruled events: If Hannah had had a son at an earlier date she would not have placed him in the Shiloh temple, to grow up there to be a man of God in the public gaze, ready for leadership."[27] Also, "God's promise is that rejoicing comes in the morning. It may come on the morning after you've wept and pled with God for his help. Or it may be the morning after wrestling and consecration, when you put your all on the altar for the Lord to use. However, it may not be until the morning of resurrection glory when the Lord returns and we see Him as He is. BUT there will be a morning of rejoicing so be of good cheer and don't give up; *"Weeping may remain for a night but rejoicing comes in the morning."* Psalm 30:5[28]

What powerful examples! Come with me now as we look through the pages of church history and glean courage and hope as we look at the examples of unsung suffering heroes of faith!

"When you reach rock bottom don't be afraid because at the bottom is the rock."

Author unknown

CHAPTER 10
INSPIRATIONAL CHARACTERS FROM CHURCH HISTORY

I've been completely encouraged by these character's examples. I've learned so much from them! From studying their lives I've gained so much. They are true role models to me and I hope they will bless you too!

SOJOURNER TRUTH

Sojourner was born into a slave family around 1797. Her birth name was Isabella. Their living conditions were awful and all they had to sleep on were wooden pallets. Her other siblings had either died or been sold into slavery.

At age eleven, she was sold into slavery to Mr & Mrs Neely. Here she was beaten violently. "Belle found her master heating some metal rods over red-hot coals. Without offering any explanation, Mr Neely grabbed Belle's hands and tied them together. He tore Belle's shirt off her back and began to beat the girl's back with rods. Belle pleaded with her master to stop and called out to God for help. Finally, she fainted. Belle lay in the straw, soaked with her own blood, and wept bitterly."[29]

Later in life her new masters forced her to marry a fellow slave called Tom. She worked hard and becoming a mother made it more difficult. "Sometimes she strapped one of her children to her back as she hoed a field."[30] Even though Belle eventually became free of slavery she then faced opposition because she was a woman and she was coloured.

In 1843 Belle decided to become a travelling evangelist, Belle was completely illiterate and could neither read nor write. "Throughout her life, she had been a victim of oppression. She had been despised because of her race and ignored because she was a woman. Now at age 46, she was dedicated to eliminating human suffering and speaking out against slavery."[31] Belle believed God had called her to leave her unhappy life, begin a dangerous mission and speak for him.

At this point she changed her name as a symbol of leaving her former life of slavery to begin a new life as God's pilgrim. Belle had memorized all the scriptures that she'd ever heard and she recalled Psalm 39:12. The word 'Sojourner' which means 'temporary resident' was a good name for God's pilgrim. "To Belle, Sojourner was a good name for someone whom God had called to travel up and down the land, showing the people their sins and being a sign to them."[32] The surname, 'Truth' came from John 8:32. She declared "I've only got one master now... his name is Truth... from this day I will walk in the light of his truth."[33]

One man called Putnam said of Sojourner: "She will often speak with an ability that surprises the educated and refined. She possesses a mind of rare power... But the truly Christian spirit that pervades all she says endears her to all who know her. Though she has suffered all the ills of slavery, she forgives all who have wronged her most freely."[34]

In one address, Sojourner said these inspiring words: "We have all been thrown down so low that nobody thought we'd ever get up again, but we have been long enough trodden now; we will come up again, and now here I am."[35]

The fact that God takes our disabilities and clothes them with supernatural strength really struck me about this next point. God truly uses weakness for his glory.

"Sojourner's illiteracy limited her opportunities for leadership. She never became part of a decision-making inner circles of either the abolitionist's or women's rights... Also, her illiteracy kept Sojourner poor because it limited her job opportunities. But, her overwhelming faith that God had called her to a special mission to set the world right side up seemed to convince Sojourner that her illiteracy was another God-given trait, like her blackness and womanhood, which fashioned her beautifully to carry out her mission."[36]

There truly is no such a thing as a disability in God's eyes!

A lady called Olive Gilbert was later given the task of penning Sojourner's autobiography. Sojourner dictated every word. The book was printed in 1850 as "The narrative of Sojourner Truth: A Northern Slave." She sold her books wherever she spoke to spread the truth. Even living in a day where ministers believed and preached that women were inferior to men didn't stop Sojourner reaching out to others and striving to get rid of slavery.

"By the beginning of 1882, Sojourner became gravely ill. Painful ulcers covered her arms and legs and she became too weak to get up from her bed. She remained this way for the next year and a half... Even in her pain and close to death, Sojourner was able to display that spirit that had become so familiar to her admirers and friends. She seemed completely at ease with her imminent death,"[37] Sojourner was even found singing hymns while lying in bed in pain, she died on November 26th 1883. Though what a legacy she left behind. All through her life she continually ignored personal hardship in the pursuit of freedom for blacks and women. "Deeply devoted to turning the world 'right side up,' she travelled far and wide to leave an inspiring legacy to all those who face a long and difficult journey for justice and respect."[38]

What a woman! Despite everything she came through, she coped in an exemplary way. May we also follow in her footsteps!

The next person that I've drawn strength from is:

MARGARET BAXTER (1639 - 1681)

"In 1644, Margaret Charlton, aged just five years old cowered with fear as Parliamentarian troops sacked her home... Little Margaret witnessed part of the castle burned to the ground, men killed, and all of the inhabitants, including herself and her family, terrorized and stripped of their clothing. Memories of this terrible incident haunted her for the rest of her life."[39]

In 1659, she became critically ill; she was at death's door yet people prayed for her round the clock. Margaret was wonderfully healed and she firmly believed it was her faithful prayer warriors that made the difference. "After recovering from her critical illness she was left with a legacy of regular severe headaches and severe respiratory problems. It is not altogether surprising that Margaret was often depressed, tense and fearful."[40] This changed though when she married preacher Richard Baxter in 1662. "Marriage to Richard transformed Margaret's social and economic status for the worse. Instead of wealth she faced persecution and insecurity. But she was overwhelmingly happy... Her depression lifted...Wherever they lived, Margaret made a great impression through her thoughtfulness and kindness. Always popular with her neighbours because of her generosity, she also showed concern for their spiritual well-being, and gave away literally hundreds of books to any who would read them."[41]

TURMOIL

"In 1664 the Conventicle Act banned all religious meetings that did not use the Prayer Book where there were five people in addition to a single family. During one private 'service' a bullet was fired through the window, narrowly missing one woman's head."[42] Richard Baxter was arrested when he refused to take the non-resistance oath and was sentenced to six months in prison. I found Margaret's reaction to this amazing! "Margaret insisted on joining him in prison... she did her best to make the prison accommodation more pleasant and 'homelike.'"[43] What a reaction! Talk about making the best of a bad situation!

CONTINUED KINDNESS

"At first they rented a section of a poor farmer's house. It was miserably smoky and Margaret's breathing problems were exacerbated... Even here, Margaret's characteristic generosity surfaced, and she managed to give the poor land lady money for an apprenticeship for her son."[44] She was willing to spend all the little that they had to relieve the deep needs around them."[45]

EATING DISORDER

Several of Margaret's friends and family had died of cancer and Margaret became sorely afraid of it. "It was fear of cancer that led her to starve herself. For many years she would only allow herself a little milk or water with some chocolate in it morning and night, with a few pieces of meat at dinner time."[46] Despite this Margaret was competent and capable... Her popularity with her neighbours was due to her cheerfulness and pleasant demeanour, which she managed to keep up even when consumed with anxiety... She was not tempted to anger, and always spoke calmly and gently."[47]

OVERSTRETCHED RESOURCES

"Margaret tended to take on too much: she was not always wise in realizing her limitations, and this could lead to anxiety and exhaustion. Richard wrote that she spent all she had for God... Her desire for usefulness overtook her strength."[48]

HER LEGACY

Margaret may have been prone to anxiety and fear, may have suffered from nightmares and had an eating disorder and may have been a perfectionist who drove herself to the limit. However, despite living in cruel times: "We see... a woman who made a conscious decision to turn away from living for herself, who decided to follow Christ and... spent all her energy... in the service of others... She did not complain at the hardships of being the wife of a nonconformist minister..."[49]

Margaret struck me as a powerful example of someone who despite her natural fearfulness put Christ first. The verse that came to my mind as I thought about her was 1 Corinthians 1:27; *"But God hath chosen the foolish things of the world to confound the wise; and God hath chosen the weak things of the world to confound the things which are mighty."*

The last character that has touched my life is:

ANNE STEELE (1717 – 1778)

ILL HEALTH

Anne was born into a wealthy family. They were also a strong Christian family and were connected with the Baptist Chapel. However, illness is no respecter of persons.

Anne was just fourteen when illness first struck. "Chronic malaria would have had a progressively debilitating effect on Anne, the major consequences of which would have been anaemia, weakness and susceptibility to other infections. It also caused fits associated with high fever, and left Anne vulnerable to consumption. For the rest of her life, Anne never enjoyed any sustained periods of good health and was often in great pain. She also seems to have suffered from terrible stomach pain and from agonizing toothache."[50] Anne's stepmother proved very faithful in nursing her through her sicknesses.

Regarding her illness, "Anne came to believe that this was a means of bringing her closer to God: she was forced to rely on him in prayer. In the early years she had to fight to maintain trust in the sovereignty of God; in later years she came to a calm, resigned contentment."[51]

In 1762 she wrote: "It was a good saying of Doctor Watts in his sickness, The Business of a Christian is to bear the will of God as well as to do it."[52]

TRIUMPHING OVER

"Anne's life was characterized by a consistent gratitude for God's goodness, a steady desire to experience his presence and a realistic sense of the temporary nature of earthly things."[53] "Cheerfulness was the key note of Anne's character. She aimed to give pleasure to those around her, even when she was suffering herself... Her humility enabled her to be patient through suffering. She did not grow resentful; she did not think that she 'deserved' a more comfortable life. Polly (her niece) described how, in extreme sickness, she was still more concerned for others. In agony attentive ... anxious still for others happiness... Anne demonstrated that even in suffering, a Christian can experience true happiness and contentment."[54]

Two volumes of her hymns and poems were published during her lifetime. Despite her suffering her faith and sense of humour kept her positive even through times of intense pain. Anne's hymns are still sung today in Baptist circles. One in particular has encouraged me so much. The following is the last three verses of this great hymn.

MY GOD, MY FATHER, BLISSFUL NAME

What'er thy sacred will ordains,
O give me strength to bear;
And let me know my Father reigns,
And trust his tender care.

If pain and sickness rend this frame,
And life almost depart,
Is not thy mercy still the same,
To cheer this drooping heart?

If cares and sorrows me surround,
Their power why should I fear?
My inward peace they cannot wound,
If thou, my God are near.[55]

From the age of fifty-four until her death six years later she was housebound yet she never grew resentful and continued to write as a means to bless others and encourage them in God.

Truly these three women give us much food for thought in coping with our own trials. Until I began my research I'd never even heard of these three women. They are unsung heroines of faith, living testimonies of how life can't put limits on the Christian's usefulness and I look up to them aspiring that my reactions to every storm would also bring glory to God.

"Diamonds cannot be polished without friction, neither can the child of God be perfected without trials."

Elizabeth George

CHAPTER 11
LITTLE LADYBIRD

My journey continues. To date this year (2009) has been a massive struggle health wise. My seasons of brief reprieve have been briefer and I've found myself thrown down even more often. On one of my good days this year I learned a lesson from a little ladybird. I've written a poem about it.

LITTLE LADYBIRD

Little ladybird. I watched you today, struggle, strive and try to break free.
A pane of glass separated you from the sunshine like prison bars
    without a key.
Each time you tried to climb up you fell almost immediately.
There you lay with your legs in the air,
    wanting to be rescued so desperately.

You were so near yet so far.
Near enough to see blue skies but nowhere near the sweet
    resting place of a flower.
Were you at the end of your rope when I stumbled in?
    Was it like a pitch black night without a star?
You kept trying and trying like a valiant soldier
    but alas weakness sapped your power.

I reached down and lifted you and felt you scurry about inside my hand.
Did you panic as the darkness and clamminess of my hand snatched
    away your hope of once again enjoying the beauty of the land?
Little did you know that your trial was about to end.
    Your storm about to be calmed.
There you went into the thick blades of grass,
    free again from pain's fierce demand.

I felt like you little ladybird as I watched you today.
For years this illness has left me feeling like I'm so near yet so far,
    like I'm in this place to stay.
You've shown me that God's strong hand will lift me up.
    His time will be perfect and he won't delay.

A place of full healing, beauty and blessing is coming soon
to little old me, one of God's little jars of clay.

Joanne's Journal

Earlier on when I was in the kitchen I spotted a little ladybird. She was
trapped inside and was desperately trying to get out. She climbed to the
window only to fall down repeatedly and have to start again. I watched
her for a moment and then I picked her up. I felt her struggling in the
darkness of my hand to get free. Then I took her outside, released her
and watched her scurry away into freedom. I felt like that little ladybird
today. For all my days of feeling so trapped, for all my days of striving
and wondering if my illness would ever slightly improve, for all the days
when I'd wondered if my life still had purpose and I struggled with being
housebound, God has stepped in today and just like I lifted the ladybird
he's lifted me and gave me a glimpse of hope, beauty and release. I can
truly declare: *"Behold God is my salvation; I will trust and not be afraid:
for the Lord JEHOVAH is my strength and my song; he also is become my
salvation."* Isaiah 12:2

That episode encouraged me so much!

During one of my bad spells this year something from God's word really
struck me. It was Elisha's call. *"He... found Elisha the son of Shaphat, who
was ploughing... and Elijah passed by him, and cast his mantle upon him."* 1
Kings 19:19-21

What struck me about this? Elisha was doing something so ordinary and
mundane. He was being faithful in doing the task at hand. He was so
willing when God called him.

My life feels mundane at the moment. I'm ploughing through a slow battle
with an illness that won't go away. It's hard work to stay on top of it and
keep hopeful. Today's passage is a reminder that I'm to keep ploughing on
even when it's frustrating, even when I don't seem to be getting anywhere,
even through seemingly wasted years. I know that someday my life will
change dramatically but for now the Lord's reminding me that I'm right in
the palm of his hand where I am and I'm to press through for his glory!

MY MINI-MIRACLE

In one of my worst spells this year my hope started to dwindle and my courage started to fade. I had been reading Galatians 4:28; *"Now we ... are the children of promise."* When I read it I felt that the Lord couldn't possibly see me as being full of promise. At this point my future prospects didn't look promising at all. However something awesome happened that night. The Lord truly got my attention.

Joanne's Journal

The most amazing and astonishing thing just happened tonight. I'm overwhelmed with a precious sense of being loved by the Lord. He didn't give up on me over these past few weeks when I've lost heart in fighting. He's stepped in completely unexpectantly.

The doorbell went this evening at 9.00 p.m. I was lying in bed. My mother answered the door and there stood a complete stranger holding a bin liner wrapped up in brown parcel tape asking for me. He said he was just delivering the parcel for someone. After he'd gone I opened it. Inside there was a brilliant new devotional book, a book about Martin Luther called 'A Mighty Fortress Is Our God', a book of Psalms, a couple of posters with verses on them and a box of malteasers! I was so shocked. I got an even bigger surprise when I saw an envelope inside the book that contained one hundred pounds. There was no name on the card at all but the verse printed on a little leaflet said: *"Faithful is he that calleth you, who will also do it."* 1 Thessalonians 5:24

I'm completely blown away. I'm humbled and awestruck. I've poured out my heart in pure thanksgiving to my Lord. It's all his grace and love. I've been at my weakest physically, emotionally and spiritually the past few weeks yet his strength has been made perfect in my weakness. I've surrendered everything afresh to him. According to his will be it unto me. I knew such a sweet calm as I abided in God and heard his still small voice whispering "You're my child of promise." Just like every one of God's children is a child of promise.

There's an awesome sense of expectancy in me tonight that things are radically going to change for the better. What an amazing God I have, everything in that package was pregnant with meaning to me. Even down to the malteasers which are my ultimate favourite sweets! The other verse in the package read: 2 Corinthians 8:9 *"For ye know the grace of our Lord Jesus Christ, that though he was rich, yet for your sakes he became poor, that ye through his poverty might be rich."*

Through my physical poverty I too am becoming rich in God! His will is unfolding in my life. Hallelujah!"

I wrote this poem when I was awestruck by my miraculous God.

MIRACULOUS GOD

M - Majestic God who we gladly serve.
You show your glory and power.
You open eyes blinded to you.
Upon us your amazing love you shower.

I - Incredible things you've done in our lives.
Nothings too hard for you. Nothing at all.
From saving to healing to unseen problems,
In your appointed time you answer when upon your name we call.

R - Rescuer of hearts in pain and torment.
One touch from your hand floods hearts with hope.
Dark moments and unsolvable nightmares flee,
When from off the cliff edge you throw a safety rope.

A - Abba Father like a child you cradle us.
With tear stained eyes we look to you to make things right.
That's what fathers do. They fix the unfixable.
You step in when we're weak and for us you fight.

C - Compassionate Lord, you see our wounds.
You intervene and bind them up,
With nail scarred hands so gently and tenderly,
You restore our lives and refill our cup.

L - Lightning flashes, fireworks sparkle.
They light up the sky in a colourful show.
Miracles that come from your hands light up our worlds.
Then we emerge stronger in you with a radiant glow.

E - El-Shaddai – You're the God of plenty who has no favourites.
The greatest miracle is in knowing you. You're our rich reward.
Let miracles and revival abound more and more,
Because everything's possible with you O Lord!

For any of you reading this who are in dire straits at the minute, keep holding tight to our miraculous God for he's no fair weather friend, he's walking this difficult path with you.

I was greatly encouraged by Isaiah 28:28-29 this summer; *"Bread corn is bruised: because he will not ever be threshing it, nor break it with the wheel of his cart, nor bruise it with his horsemen. This also cometh forth from the Lord of hosts which is wonderful in counsel, and excellent in working."* Another translation, NIV renders it: *"Bread corn is bruised ... no one crushes it forever."* Grain is first beaten and bruised until they crumble to pieces even then the grinding and beating process continues until at last the powder is fine enough to be used for baking the best bread. In the same way although bread corn is bruised no one crushes it forever, only until the broken grain is ready for its highest use. I won't be bruised forever, just like the bread corn there's a much higher purpose in all this refining. I may feel tonight that I just can't take anymore sickness but this encourages me to remember that this is only for a season. I won't go through more than I can bear for my Lord is too compassionate to allow that. He'll give me his strength to endure.

I'm going to anticipate newness of life tonight. I've already read Deuteronomy 32:39 today and it's encouraged my heart so much. *"See now that I, even I, am he, and there is no god with me: I kill, and I make alive; I wound, and I heal: neither is there any that can deliver out of my hand."*

As I thought about this I worshipped God. He's really strengthened his drooping flower tonight. Heavenly streams of refreshing have flooded my soul.

NEWNESS OF LIFE

Newness of life.
Being birthed from my strife.
After years of being under the master surgeon's knife.
It's the feeling of excitement and expectancy
    that precedes a maiden becoming a wife.

Newness of life springing up within me.
I'm going from winter to spring with a heart filled with glee.
It's a God appointed season. Like a prisoner released I'll be free.
After walking in darkness for so long,
    with my own eyes daybreak I shall see.

Newness of life, covering me like heaven's blanket.
The haze is lifting, fears are dispelled. I've no reason to fret.
I stand in awe of God, to his mercy and love I'm in debt.
Mine eyes are ever toward the Lord; for he shall pluck my feet out of the net.
Psalm 25:15

My heart's overflowing tonight. I don't know when my appointed time for healing will come but I do know that newness of life is on its way. I haven't got a clue when but I know it will come to pass.

When I think of newness of life many pretty pictures come into my mind. The first green buds appearing on the trees after a long winter. A mother holding her newborn baby so carefully knitted together with so much potential. New born lambs struggling to stand up while nestled close to their mother's for warmth. A butterfly emerging from a cocoon. A child on their first day of school standing proudly in their little uniform holding a brand new lunchbox. A bride radiant on her wedding day. When I picture newness of life in my own circumstance I picture a body that works in the way that it's meant to, a deeper walk with God and a desire to dedicate all to him. I'm holding onto Isaiah 43:19; *"Behold, I will do a new thing; now it shall spring forth; shall ye not know it? I will even make a way in the wilderness, and rivers in the desert."*

The Lord is doing a new thing in me. Old physical capabilities may have gone for now but he is ushering in something beautiful. I'm confident that God will make a way in my wilderness and send rivers of refreshing to my desert. I don't know if this newness of life will fit in with what I want it to look like. I don't know if it will take a few months or a few years or if perfect healing won't come till I'm in glory with God but this I do know, the one who has declared me as a new creation when I gave him my life is working in me now bringing to pass his creative purpose and no amount of barriers or apparent obstacles will stop him. For nothing, absolutely nothing is impossible for my God. The only way forward for me now is to keep walking in newness of life even when things are rocky, when the pain makes my heart bleed, when I'm surrounded by apparent deadness and dead ends, when loneliness and isolation are my only companions I need to keep marching forward. I want my relationship with the Lord to be new and fresh everyday. I don't want to stagnate and try and live off previous blessings or sermons that I've heard the week before.

I long to be walking in harmony with God. My part in this newness of life is to keep moving nearer to his heart. One night two years ago I was really fighting exhaustion. Exhaustion had prevented me sensing the Lord's nearness even though I was trying to pray. The next day I wrote a song called "In Tune With Heaven." It's based on the instance in Song of Solomon where the girl wakes up to the sound of her beloved knocking at her door but by the time she got up he was gone. Song Of Solomon 3:1-4 says; *"By night on my bed I sought him whom my soul loveth: I sought him, but I found him not. I will rise now, and go about the city in the streets and in the broad ways I will seek him whom my soul loveth: I sought him but I found him not... It was but a little that I passed from them, but I found him... I held him and would not let him go..."*

I have found the one that my soul loves and come what may I'm not letting go.

IN TUNE WITH HEAVEN

I awake to a breaking heart.
My beloved where have you gone?
Like the girl in Song of Songs I've missed you.
Missed you knocking at my heart's door.

Now I'm desperate for your closeness, desperate for your touch, desperate to be restored to you my first love.

CHORUS

In tune with heaven let me be.
In tune with you my Darling Lord.
This is my longing, my desire, my plea.
Take all my carnal fleshly moods, my wrong desires and attitudes.
In tune with heaven, in tune with you, this is my cry.

There's no point in living without you.
My beloved I'm seeking you.
Winter's past, the rain is over. Take me into springtime with you.
I'm tired of living my own way. I only care about your will,
Let me die to self today and revive my heart I pray.

Set me as a seal upon your heart.
My beloved purify me.
Many waters can't quench your love for me.
Let my heartbeat, beat in time with yours.
A reflection of your beauty is all I long to be.
A channel of blessing, a life abandoned to you.

I have hope in the Lord that I love so much. He has given me many promises but the promise of his unfailing love is what is sustaining me right now. His love is not dependent on our status or capabilities; he lavishes it upon us freely. A few years ago I was looking after a child. He was totally stunning. As I looked at him I thought 'I love you so much yet you've done nothing to make me love you except just being your own gorgeous self.' That's a lesson that I'm still trying to learn. We equate our worth with our doings whereas the Lord equates our worth with our simply being. He delights in the work of his hands before we even do anything. Just like I loved that baby so much that's how much the Lord loves us. If you know the one that my soul loves, determine to let nothing hinder you from moving forward into newness of life even in your pain. He is the one who promises the beauty of "a fir tree for the thorns and a myrtle tree for life's briars." If you don't know my Lord please don't delay in coming to him.

He is our only hope in this world for time with all its tests and for eternity. Let him pour his healing balm into your soul and walk with you, let him pour his strength into you as you journey through. From Isaiah 55:13.

"**Whatever my lot thou hast caused me to say,
blessed hope it is well with my soul.**"

Horatio Spafford 1873

Joanne Peden can be contacted at amyrtletree@hotmail.com

Notes

1 *Matthew Henry Commentary* (USA 1991), p1205.
2 *Matthew Henry Commentary* (USA 1991), p1205.
3 *Believer's Bible Commentary* (Nashville 1995), p1371.
4 Francena H. Arnold, *Not My Will* (Chicago 1991), p189.
5 *Life Application Bible NIV* (Illinois 1992), p1741.
6 Warren W. Wiersbe, *Life Sentences* (Michigan 2007), p289.
7 *New Bible Commentary* (England 2008), p1259.
8 Warren W. Wiersbe, *Life Sentences* (Michigan 2007), p291.
9 *New Bible Commentary* (England 2008), p1091.
10 *New Bible Commentary* (England 2008), pp1104-5.
11 Warren W. Wiersbe, *Life Sentences* (Michigan 2007), p284.
12 Warren W. Wiersbe, *Life Sentences* (Michigan 2007), p285.
13 *Believer's Bible Commentary* (Nashville 1995), p1602.
14 *New Bible Commentary* (England 2008), p1078.
15 *New Bible Commentary* (England 2008), p1078.
16 Warren W. Wiersbe, *Life Sentences* (Michigan 2007), p287.
17 Warren W. Wiersbe, *Life Sentences* (Michigan 2007), p287.
18 *New Bible Commentary* (England 2008), p289.
19 Warren W. Wiersbe, *Life Sentences* (Michigan 2007), p117.
20 *New Bible Commentary* (England 2008), p291. check
21 Warren W. Wiersbe, *Life Sentences* (Michigan 2007), p118.
22 Warren W. Wiersbe, *Life Sentences* (Michigan 2007), p124.
23 *New Bible Commentary* (England 2008), p298.
24 Warren W. Wiersbe, *Life Sentences* (Michigan 2007), p124.
25 *Life Application Bible NIV* (Illinois 1992), p430.
26 *New Bible Commentary* (England 2008), p298.
27 *New Bible Commentary* (England 2008), p299.
28 Warren W. Wiersbe, *Life Sentences* (Michigan 2007), p126-127.
29 W. Terry Whalin "Sojourner Truth," in *Inspiring Women of the Faith*, p14 (USA 2008).
30 W. Terry Whalin "Sojourner Truth," in *Inspiring Women of the Faith*, p19 (USA 2008).
31 W. Terry Whalin "Sojourner Truth," in *Inspiring Women of the Faith*, p41 (USA 2008).
32 W. Terry Whalin "Sojourner Truth," in *Inspiring Women of the Faith*, p38 (USA 2008).
33 W. Terry Whalin "Sojourner Truth," in *Inspiring Women of the Faith*, p39 (USA 2008).
34 W. Terry Whalin "Sojourner Truth," in *Inspiring Women of the Faith*, p52 (USA 2008).
35 W. Terry Whalin "Sojourner Truth," in *Inspiring Women of the Faith*, p58 (USA 2008).
36 W. Terry Whalin "Sojourner Truth," in *Inspiring Women of the Faith*, p73 (USA 2008).
37 W. Terry Whalin "Sojourner Truth," in *Inspiring Women of the Faith*, p82 (USA 2008).
38 W. Terry Whalin "Sojourner Truth," in *Inspiring Women of the Faith*, p83 (USA 2008).
39 Sharon James, *In Trouble and In Joy*, (England 2003), p27.
40 Sharon James, *In Trouble and In Joy*, (England 2003), p30.
41 Sharon James, *In Trouble and In Joy*, (England 2003), pp35-6.
42 Sharon James, *In Trouble and In Joy*, (England 2003), p38.
43 Sharon James, *In Trouble and In Joy*, (England 2003), pp38-9.
44 Sharon James, *In Trouble and In Joy*, (England 2003), p39.
45 Sharon James, *In Trouble and In Joy*, (England 2003), p49.
46 Sharon James, *In Trouble and In Joy*, (England 2003), p46.
47 Sharon James, *In Trouble and In Joy*, (England 2003), pp48-9.
48 Sharon James, *In Trouble and In Joy*, (England 2003), pp51-2.
49 Sharon James, *In Trouble and In Joy*, (England 2003), p52.

50 Sharon James, *In Trouble and In Joy*, (England 2003), p125.
51 Sharon James, *In Trouble and In Joy*, (England 2003), p139.
52 Sharon James, *In Trouble and In Joy*, (England 2003), p139.
53 Sharon James, *In Trouble and In Joy*, (England 2003), p137.
54 Sharon James, *In Trouble and In Joy*, (England 2003), pp147-8.
55 Sharon James, *In Trouble and In Joy*, (England 2003), p163.

Bibliography

Arnold, Francena H. *Not My Will*
(Chicago, Moody Press, 1991)

Bingham, Derick. *The Bronte's: Veins Running Fire*
(Belfast, Ambassador, 2007)

Carson, D.A., France, R.T., Motyer, J.A. and Wenham, G.J. (eds)., *New Bible Commentary* (England, IVP, 2008)

Henry, Matthew. *Matthew Henry's Commentary*
(USA, Hendrickson Publishers, 1991)

James, Sharon. *In Trouble And In Joy*
(England, Evangelical Press, 2003)

Lewis, Beverley. *Abram's Daughters*
(USA, Bethany House Publishers, 2002)

Life Application Bible NIV
(Wheaton, Illinois Tyndale House Publishers, 1991)

McDonald, William and Farstad, Art (e.d.), *Believers' Bible Commentary*
(USA, Thomas Nelson Publishing, 1995)

Wiersbe, Warren. *Life Sentences*
(Grand Rapids Michigan, Zondervan, 2007)

Wellman, Sam and Whalin, W. Terry., *Inspiring Women Of The Faith*
(USA, Barbour Publishing, 2008)